WICCA

TREE MAGIC

A Wiccan's Guide and Grimoire for Working Magic with Trees, with Tree Spells and Magical Crafts

LISA CHAMBERLAIN

Wicca Tree Magic

Copyright © 2019 by Lisa Chamberlain.

Published by **Chamberlain Publications**

ISBN-13: 978-1-912715-03-9

Disclaimer

No part of this publication may be reproduced or transmitted in any form or by any means, mechanical or electronic, including photocopying or recording, or by any information storage and retrieval system, or transmitted by email without permission in writing from the publisher.

While all attempts have been made to verify the information provided in this publication, neither the author nor the publisher assumes any responsibility for errors, omissions, or contrary interpretations of the subject matter herein.

This book is for entertainment purposes only. The views expressed are those of the author alone, and should not be taken as expert instruction or commands. The reader is responsible for his or her own actions.

Adherence to all applicable laws and regulations, including international, federal, state, and local governing professional licensing, business practices, advertising, and all other aspects of doing business in the US, Canada, or any other jurisdiction is the sole responsibility of the purchaser or reader.

Neither the author nor the publisher assumes any responsibility or liability whatsoever on the behalf of the purchaser or reader of these materials.

Any perceived slight of any individual or organization is purely unintentional.

YOUR FREE GIFT

Thank you for adding this book to your Wiccan library! To learn more, why not join Lisa's Wiccan community and get an exclusive, free spell book?

The book is a great starting point for anyone looking to try their hand at practicing magic. The ten beginner-friendly spells can help you to create a positive atmosphere within your home, protect yourself from negativity, and attract love, health, and prosperity.

Little Book of Spells is now available to read on your laptop, phone, tablet, Kindle or Nook device!

To download, simply visit the following link:

www.wiccaliving.com/bonus

GET THREE
FREE AUDIOBOOKS
FROM LISA CHAMBERLAIN

Did you know that all of Lisa's books are available in audiobook format? Best of all, you can get **three audiobooks completely free** as part of a 30-day trial with Audible.

Wicca Starter Kit contains three of Lisa's most popular books for beginning Wiccans, all in one convenient place. It's the best and easiest way to learn more about Wicca while also taking audiobooks for a spin! Simply visit:

www.wiccaliving.com/free-wiccan-audiobooks

Alternatively, *Spellbook Starter Kit* is the ideal option for building your magical repertoire using candle and color magic, crystals and mineral stones, and magical herbs. Three spellbooks —over 150 spells—are available in one free volume, here:

www.wiccaliving.com/free-spell-audiobooks

Audible members receive free audiobooks every month, as well as exclusive discounts. It's a great way to experiment and see if audiobook learning works for you.

If you're not satisfied, you can cancel anytime within the trial period. You won't be charged, and you can still keep your books!

CONTENTS

INTRODUCTION

For many Witches, Druids, and other Pagans, there is no earthly manifestation more sacred than a tree. Anyone who has ever had the good fortune to find themselves standing in a forest can attest to the peaceful, almost other-worldly feeling of watching tall branches sway in the breeze, the sunlight flickering as it's filtered through a canopy of bright green leaves.

But the magical energy of trees can be felt wherever they grow, whether it be a forest, a jungle, a meadow, a desert, or a mountain ridge. In fact, this magic can be found among the trees in your neighborhood park and in your own back yard. All you need to do is tune in to their silent, graceful presence.

Trees have been partners to humanity's well-being since the beginning of human existence, both on the physical and spiritual levels. Not only have we prospered from using their lumber, their fruits and nuts, and their medicinal components, but scientists have also discovered less visible benefits of simply being near trees, such as improved focus, stress reduction, and better emotional health.

These recent discoveries hint at something that Witches have always known—trees emit powerful energies that affect not only us, but the entire Universe. Working consciously with these energies to shape the conditions of our lives is one way of practicing the ancient art of magic.

Trees are perhaps the most diverse natural sources of magical ingredients. Depending on your style and your intent, you might make use of the leaves, bark, or branches of a tree in your spellwork, or take advantage of the magical properties of the nuts or fruits it provides. You might work with particular tree resins or essences, or utilize their energies in incense or essential oils. Some trees have even been the source of what we normally call "crystals" or "mineral stones," like jet and amber, which have been used in magic since ancient times.

Of course, you can also accomplish some astounding manifestations simply by sitting at the base of a tree and attuning to its majestic presence. In fact, even just gazing at images of trees can have a magical effect on your personal energy. As you can see, the practice of tree magic has endless potential!

This guide is intended to provide a solid grounding in the art of working magic with trees. In Part One, we'll explore the magical significance of trees to our pagan ancestors, as well as to the contemporary practice of Wicca, which draws on those older traditions. Part Two offers advice for forging and deepening a personal connection with the trees that live near you. Here, you'll also find profiles of 13 common magical trees—their history and lore, their energetic properties, and their magical uses. Part 3 contains an "arboreal grimoire" of sorts, featuring spells, meditations, rituals, and recipes for working with the natural magic of trees. A table of correspondences for easy reference is also included at the back of the book.

A note about the trees selected for inclusion in this guide:

Much of the lore about tree magic found in contemporary Wiccan and other Neopagan practices has been handed down from European pagan traditions. Many trees, such as rowan, ash, and oak, were revered by the Celts, the Norse, and other ancient European cultures. As a result, many modern sources on tree magic are focused on species native to Europe, where these traditions originate. This makes perfect sense, of course, and it works well for practitioners who live in European countries.

For those practicing in the United States* and Canada, however, there can be a slight sense of disconnect when working from descriptions and images of trees that grow on a different continent. Therefore, this guide takes a slightly unusual approach, focusing on trees native to North America**, to help the Witches of "the New World" ground their practice of tree magic more firmly on home soil.

By and large, the trees featured here can be considered the North American "cousins" to those found most often in traditional European lore. For example, the venerable yew tree found throughout Europe is somewhat different in appearance from the Pacific yew, which is native to the northern Pacific coast from California to Alaska. The accompanying illustrations are also based on common North American species.

As for the lore and magical associations covered in this guide, most are still largely derived from European traditions, with exceptions made for trees like maple and cedar, whose magical history is more rooted in practices of North American indigenous peoples.

May you find knowledge, guidance, insight, and inspiration for your journey in the pages that follow.

Blessed Be.

****

Apologies to Hawaiian readers, for whom a completely separate section on native magical trees would be required!

** *"North America" is defined in this guide as the U.S. and Canada.*

PART ONE

TREES AND THE OLD RELIGION

OUR
INDISPENSIBLE FRIENDS

We all know that humans, as well as animals, plants, and insects, depend heavily on trees for basic survival. Trees provide food for a whole host of living things, both visible and invisible, and shelter for humans and animals alike. In fact, our earliest ancestors lived in trees!

As humans evolved, trees became the chief source of fuel for fire, thus providing a crucial turning point toward civilization. And before people began to build their own permanent shelters, trees often served as the only available cover from pelting rain and the fierce heat of the sun.

The bark, leaves, berries, and sap of many trees were used for medicine and healing, while fruits and nuts provided daily sustenance. Twigs, branches, and stumps were transformed into tools, and carved into toys for children. Humans may have "climbed down" from the trees in the course of our evolution, but it's clear that we didn't leave them behind.

As time went on, trees were used to build homes, make furniture and paper, and many other objects of daily life that we now take for granted. Thanks to modern technology, we can now eat the fruits and nuts of an astounding variety of trees from all around the world. We can also harness the healing power of trees in new ways, through flower and bark essences and essential oils. Of course, we still rely on trees for very basic needs as well—we need them to produce oxygen, help clear pollutants from the air, and hold the soil together along the banks of creeks and rivers.

Unfortunately, trees have been taken for granted far too often over the centuries, as humanity's capacity for both creation and destruction has continued to develop. Whether they are chopped down for the value of their wood, burned down to make way for agriculture, or cleared to build endless housing developments, whole forests of trees have been disappearing all over the globe at a rate that many people believe threatens the future of human survival.

This dilemma presents an interesting irony—trees helped us advance to the point where we can now destroy enough of them to ultimately destroy ourselves. It's a profound example of the energetic imbalance in our species' relationship with Nature.

Many Wiccans and other modern Pagans passionately believe that we as a species need to work in harmony with Nature again, and this is a large part of what draws many to the Craft. As a result, the practices of both covens and solitary Witches often incorporate working for the healing of the Earth through preserving trees and forests.

Of course, a focus on honoring the trees is not a new practice within Witchcraft and other modern Pagan traditions. As we will see below, indigenous cultures around the world have always been in tune with these life-giving beings. In particular, we'll explore the history of the spiritual relationships between trees and our European pagan ancestors, which fostered magical traditions that are still followed to this day.

We'll then examine the significance of trees in the Wiccan cosmology, from our concepts of deity to the co-creative nature of the Elements and the ever-changing seasons. Finally, we'll take a close look at how trees are incorporated into some of the most time-honored magical tools used in Wicca and other modern Pagan practices.

TREES AND PAGANS: AN ANCIENT RELATIONSHIP

The magical and spiritual significance of trees was almost certainly known to all cultures around the world from the beginning of human history. Myth and lore surrounding trees is found in every land inhabited by humans, from the Inuits of the Arctic to the Akha mountain people of Southeast Asia and the San people of the Kalahari Desert in southern Africa.

Beliefs about the nature and purpose of trees vary as widely as the cultures that have traditionally revered them, and many of these ancient beliefs are still alive today in some form. For example, in some cultures, trees are believed to have their own unique souls. In others, trees are merely homes for spirits, who can choose to inhabit them or leave them at any time. The ancient Greeks and Romans, however, believed that *hamadryads* (tree-dwelling nature spirits) would die when their trees did, whether the tree was cut down or died of natural causes.

Tree spirits might be non-human in origin, such as fairies, dryads, and other Elemental beings, or they might be the actual ancestors of the people who live near them. Several belief systems allow for deceased humans to come into their next incarnation as trees. And in many tales from ancient Greece, the gods could turn humans into trees while in their current incarnations!

Trees could also be the homes of deities, and were often associated with particular ones. For example, there is a grove in India considered sacred to the monkey god Hanuman. For the ancient Romans, oak trees were connected with Jupiter, the god of the sky, and a special fig tree in the center of Rome was sacred to Romulus, the city's mythical founder. Trees were the first temples in the religious life of many peoples, including the Greeks, the Celts, and other ancient Europeans.

Some cultures believed that trees can feel pain, and certain trees have been said to make terrible sounds when being cut down. The ancient Persians waited until trees fell naturally on their own, rather than causing them such distress. Other societies would ask for forgiveness, make substantial offerings to the tree before felling it, or consult with the community's shaman to determine whether the tree would come down willingly. The Celts believed that permission must be sought from an elder tree before cutting it down, and even then many people were still wary of doing so.

These traditions were often about more than just respect for the trees as sovereign beings—people also feared that the spirits of the tree would be angered and take revenge. Indeed, trees were not universally viewed as benevolent or harmless beings. Forests, which were unfathomably vast in many parts of the world before the onset of human modernization, show up in many myths and folktales as intimidating, dangerous, and forbidden places where evil spirits reside and unsuspecting wanderers could disappear forever.

Despite this trepidation about forests, the value of trees to human survival was widely acknowledged by the ancients around the globe. Trees stood as symbols of life, abundance, fertility, and renewal. Many belief systems include a version of the archetypal Tree of Life, including Judaism and (by association) Christianity, and artifacts depicting similar concepts are found in ancient Iran and Mesopotamia, China, and several European cultures. These depictions often feature a lush, abundant tree with many fruits, surrounded by animals. In some myths, the tree of life is literally the origin of all plant life—it is the first living plant on Earth and contains the seeds of all other plants to come.

Trees were also associated with knowledge and wisdom, such as the Bodhi tree under which the Buddha became enlightened. It is perhaps this association with wisdom that gave rise to the Kabbalah, a mystical tradition that began in Judaism and has been adapted over the centuries by both Christians and magical practitioners alike.

Visually depicted in the shape of the Tree of Life, the Kabbalah is a framework for viewing the transformation of nonphysical reality into the physical reality of the world as we know it. All of creation is represented within the "branches" of the Tree of Life, and many Witches who work with this symbolic system find that their spiritual and magical practice is enhanced by studying the Tree of Life through the lens of the Western mystery tradition.

Another symbol found widely around the globe is the World Tree. In many cultures, trees are integral parts of creation myths, and are often seen as ladders or bridges between the physical world of human beings and the invisible world of the gods. It has been theorized that this universal pattern could stem from ancient genetic memory, an acknowledgement of our earliest history as tree-dwellers, when the forest could indeed have been the whole world.

The World Tree archetype appears in belief systems from Siberia to the native tribes of North America, as well as in Chinese, Hindu, and African traditions. Some people equate the World Tree with the Tree of Life, but while they may be interchangeable in some cosmologies, in others there is a distinct difference.

The Tree of Life is a symbol of what living organisms need to survive and thrive, while the World Tree relates to everything in the Universe— the gods, spirit beings, and geographical features like mountains and rivers. The World Tree is, in many cases, the Universe itself.

NORTHERN EUROPEAN TREE WORSHIP

In the Northern European world, where many of our Neopagan traditions come from, two ancient cultures in particular are known for working with trees as a means of connecting with the divine and the magical energies present throughout the Universe: the Celts and the ancient Germanic peoples.

Since the legends, myths, and lore of both of these cultural groups was primarily oral rather than written down, much of the information we have about their beliefs and activities comes from outside observers, such as the ancient writers Tacitus and Pliny.

We also have plenty of mythology that was finally written down in later centuries, but because many of these later sources were imbued with the influence of Christianity, it's hard to know just how accurate the details of the stories are. However, we can still glean plenty of insight into how our pagan ancestors worked with the natural wisdom of the trees that grew in their native lands.

THE DRUIDS AND CELTIC MAGIC

The Celts were an ethnolinguistic group of tribes who originated in central Europe and migrated to several places on the continent and throughout the British Isles. The Druids were their spiritual and philosophical leaders, and held authority over the religious rites, education, legal matters, healing, and the oral tradition of the tribe.

According to ancient observers, as well as myths and legends largely from British and Irish sources, the Druids had several customs associated with trees. One of the most widely known is their reverence for oaks and in particular oak groves, which the Druid priests considered sacred and where they held religious rites. The word "druid" has actually been connected to an old Welsh name for "oak," and translated as "knowing the oak tree." The Druids were also most certainly magicians—so much so that in even in recent Irish history, the words "Druid" and "magician" meant the same thing.

One of the most well-known Druidic rituals involved the harvesting of mistletoe from a sacred oak. Using a sickle, the Druids would climb the tree on the sixth day of the lunar cycle, and slice a branch of mistletoe so that it fell onto a white cloak placed on the ground beneath the tree. This harvesting ritual was followed by the sacrifice of two white bulls, and then a feast.

The purpose of this practice is unclear (as is the specific role of the mistletoe), but it is a fair assumption that the bulls were offered to one or more of the gods in the ancient Celtic pantheon. Druids were said to revere mistletoe because it "fell" from the realm of the gods, and this marked the oak tree on which it grew as sacred. Mistletoe was also associated with healing powers (and has in fact been used recently as a part of treatment for cancer patients). White is said to have represented purity to the Druids, which may shed light on the use of white bulls and a white cloth, as well as another reason for the importance of mistletoe—its white berries.

Although the oak is perhaps the tree most widely associated with the Druids, it is definitely not the only one they worked with. In fact, it seems the Celts believed that all trees have spirits, and that those trees with the most palpable magical energy were inhabited by the most powerful spirits. Furthermore, each species of tree held its own type of spirit, and so one species of tree could be more suitable than another for a particular magical purpose.

These spirits would have been present in all of the trees mentioned in connection with the Druids, including rowan, hazel, yew, aspen, birch, and apple. Branches, boughs, and bark from these and other trees might be used for healing, divination, wand-making, and/or various rituals. For example, leafy birch branches were used to cover the body of the deceased as it was carried to the grave on a wooden pallet. The grave itself was measured with a rod of aspen or yew, which was inscribed with Ogham lettering (though it is unclear what the inscription may have meant).

Ogham (pronounced "OH-um") is the name of the script, or alphabet, used for writing the Irish language during the first few centuries of the Common Era (CE). Some historians assert that the alphabet was actually developed within the first century BCE or earlier, but it's hard to know since any inscriptions made on wood would have disintegrated well before Ogham was studied by scholars. At any rate, it is believed that the Druids invented this alphabet, possibly as a means of communicating in secret, so that the authorities in neighboring Roman-ruled Britain would not understand them.

Several of the letters in Ogham were named for trees—birch, alder, willow, oak, and hazel. Additionally, the ancient Irish words for "letters" was "trees" (*feda*) and "forking branches," (*nin*) appropriate names for the branch-like shapes of the letters themselves. Some people believe that the Ogham was also a system of magical symbols, as well as a form of divination, that only initiated Druids had access to. This belief has never been proven academically, but it has nevertheless inspired the practices of many modern Celtic-oriented Witches and other Pagans.

We do know for certain that the Druids used actual trees in a variety of divination methods. In one, the future was divined from the appearance of the roots of trees. In another, branches were fashioned into "omen sticks." These were cast upon the ground, and answers were extrapolated from the way they landed. (From some tales in Irish mythology, it appears that Ogham lettering may have been involved in this method, but it's unclear how the symbols would have been interpreted.) In a more elaborate divination ritual, the hides of the sacrificial bulls mentioned above were spread over a frame made from a rowan tree, with the inside of the hide facing upward, and then read for signs of upcoming events.

Wands were clearly of great significance to the Druids, who carried them in part as a signifier of their position within Celtic society. More importantly, however, wands were also used much as they are in Wiccan and other Pagan ritual and magic today: to direct energy toward a desired result.

It is also thought that Druids spoke special words, or "charms," while using the wand for magical work. Wands were made from the branches of trees, and wands made from hazel, rowan, elder, apple, and yew appear in Irish mythology as well as in Celtic folk customs, which most likely trace back to the pre-Christian days of the Druids. In the myths, wands are used for transformation—usually of a person or deity into an animal—as well as divination and defense.

In the folk traditions, some of which are still followed today, wands of hazel and rowan were used to bless and protect the home, often as part of cross-quarter day celebrations (like Beltane and Samhain). On Imbolc, or Brighid's Day in Ireland, a wand made of willow or birch was left for the goddess-turned-saint Brighid, in hopes that she would visit the household in the night.

Irish lore sheds light on many other magical traditions surrounding trees. Hawthorn blossoms were considered unlucky if brought into the house, and Beltane Eve was the only time when hawthorn branches could be harvested safely, without risking misfortune. Beltane was also a good time to harvest hazel branches for wands, as they would then have more powerful potential, particularly for protection from evil spirits. A wand of elder also had protective properties, and was associated with the fairy folk. Hazel wands were used for weather magic, as well as divining the location of water.

The fruits and nuts of sacred trees were also important in Irish myths, legends, and customs. Hazelnuts were used magically for knowledge and wisdom, and Scottish Druids were known to chew on hazelnuts on Samhain to gain prophecies about the future from the Otherworld. Acorns were eaten by the Druids of Gaul for similar purposes.

Apples are central to some of the most well-known magical traditions from the Celtic world, which is where the Halloween tradition of "bobbing for apples" originates. The game was played by young unmarried people as a fun kind of marriage divination—the first person to grab hold of an apple with their teeth would be the next one in the community to marry. Another love divination ritual called for peeling an apple in one long strip and tossing the peel to the floor to discover the first letter of a future lover's name.

Some of these beliefs and customs continue among Celtic people today. For example, it is still believed by many that fairies dwell in any place where oak, ash, and thorn trees grow together. And "wishing trees" are still in use throughout the Celtic isles.

The most well-known type of wishing trees are found growing near certain wells which are considered sacred (or "holy"). Their branches are hung with strips of cloth which represent the prayers, petitions, or magical intentions of people who tie them. These trees are traditionally whitethorn, hawthorn, or ash trees, but the tree's proximity to the well is more important than its species. The chief purposes of these wishing tree rituals are healing and fertility, though some people may tie a cloth simply to honor the spirit (or saint, for Christians) of the well.

Another type of wishing tree are the "coin trees," which are typically oak, ash, or hawthorn, whose trunks and branches are studded with coins. (These are usually trees which have already fallen down.) People press the coins into the wood for all kinds of wishes. These two wishing tree traditions are found not just in Celtic areas, but in many places around the world.

But local descendants of the Celts are not the only people who keep the ancient tree traditions alive. Modern Druids (or "Neodruids"), Witches, and other Pagans living in many places around the world have drawn substantially on Celtic myth and lore to shape their magical practices. Today's "NeoDruids," for example, may employ a wand made from an apple branch, hung with small bells in the manner of their Druid ancestors, to access the Otherworld and invite friendly spirits to join in. And many modern groups of Druids are known as "groves," whether they meet among the trees or in a member's living room.

The Ogham (mentioned above) also continues to be significant for magical practitioners who find meaning in its symbols and its association with sacred trees. Much of the modern lore about Ogham originates with a book published in the mid-20th century called *The White Goddess*, by poet Robert Graves, who suggested that the symbolic system encoded ancient esoteric wisdom which had been handed down over the centuries, ultimately arriving in the hands of Irish Druids.

Based on earlier works by Celtic scholars, as well as local folklore surrounding the trees and other plants the Ogham letters were named for, Graves and others devised a system of magical and divinatory meanings for the Ogham that are still used today. Graves is also largely responsible for the invention of the Celtic tree calendar, a 13-month calendar that begins with the Winter Solstice and has 28 days per month. Each month is named for a tree, beginning with Birch (or *Beith* in Irish) and ending with Elder (or *Ruis*).

Much of Graves' work has since been discredited by contemporary scholars, and reconstructionist Celtic Pagans generally dismiss the practices that were inspired by his theories. Nonetheless, elements of Graves' unique, imaginative work have had a substantial influence on many forms of modern Paganism—including Wicca—and are still relevant today. The same is true, of course, of the authentic lore and traditions of the Celts, particularly when it comes to working with the magic of trees.

TREES AND THE ANCIENT GERMANS

The diverse tribes collectively known as the ancient Germanic peoples, who migrated throughout the central, western, and northern areas of Europe (including much of England and parts of Ireland and Scotland), are also believed to have centered much of their religious activity around trees.

Their Roman observers noted that their religious rituals took place in groves rather than in temples, and that both groves and individual trees were often dedicated to a particular deity. Some contemporary scholars believe that the woods were indeed the first temples of the ancient Germans, and that actual structures designated for ritual purposes didn't come along until later.

Whatever the case, the religious significance of trees was clearly part of Northern European culture until well into the 2nd millennium CE, as the Christian church found itself having to "ban" certain trees due to their association with pagan ritual. In fact, the role trees played in the lives of these pagan ancestors has had a lasting influence on Western culture, which can still be detected in both Christian and secular holiday traditions today.

Much of what we know about the beliefs of the Germanic peoples comes from Norse mythology and literature. It's here that we find one of the most well-known versions of the World Tree, known as Yggdrasil. This great tree stands at the center of the Universe, and the nine worlds of the Norse cosmology are held within its roots, trunk, and branches.

All things within the Universe are connected to each other through the vast expanse of this tree. Animals, humans, mythical creatures, and gods all benefit from Yggdrasil in one way or another, as the tree runs through all the dimensions in which they dwell. Mythical creatures live within the tree, and the gods assemble there to discuss important events and watch over the worlds.

Yggdrasil is particularly associated with the concept of fate and with a kind of shamanic journeying. The Norns, the mythical female beings said to weave the world's past, present, and future, reside at the base of the World Tree and tend to its roots. Odin, the god who discovered the secrets of the magical symbols known as runes, gained this knowledge by hanging upside down from a branch of Yggdrasil for nine days and nights, until he grasped their hidden meanings. These and other stories within Norse mythology show how trees were viewed as intermediaries between the world of humans and the spirit worlds.

Traditionally, the World Tree has been believed to be an ash tree, and is translated as such in all of the myths in which it appears. However, many scholars have reason to believe that Yggdrasil is actually a yew tree, and that "ash" was a mistranslation of the old myths.

For one thing, Yggdrasil is described as being an everlasting and evergreen tree. Yet the ash tree is not an evergreen, and does not live exceptionally long (most species live 100-200 years). By contrast, the yew is a conifer, staying green all year round, and can live well over 1,000 years. Furthermore, in many parts of Northern Europe, the yew has traditionally represented the Yule tree (perhaps because of its association with death and regeneration), which is seen as a symbol of Yggdrasil.

The yew is relatively modest in size, however, in comparison to the mighty ash, which can grow to heights over 100 feet, compared to the yew's typical height of 30 to 60 feet. This may partly explain why the ash was assumed to be the model for Yggdrasil.

At any rate, the ash was clearly important to the Norse, as the first man was said to be created from this tree. (The first woman was created from either an elm tree, a rowan tree, or a vine, depending on the translation from Old Norse.) Several other sacred trees are mentioned in Norse mythology as well, including Barnstokkr, which a king's hall was built around, and Glasir, which stands in the front of Valhalla, the hall where fallen warriors are welcomed into the afterlife.

Like the Druids, the ancient Norse made use of wands for ritual and magical purposes. However, the carrier of the wand in this case was typically a woman, known as a *volva*, or seeress. The *volur* (plural of volva) held an elevated place in Norse society, and would never be harmed while walking about, for they knew powerful magic, and were respected and valued (as well as somewhat feared) by their communities.

In Norse mythology, even Odin, the "Allfather," consults a volva about the future. "Volva" translates as "staff carrier," which points to the significance of the wand (a shortened version of the staff) as part of the seeress' function. She is said to sit on a special raised platform, holding her staff, and with the aid of song enter a trance, through which she then gains information from the spirit world.

Scholars believe the staff was considered a physical manifestation of the World Tree, serving to link the visible human world with the spirit realms. Compared to the Celts, there is less evidence within Norse literature that certain types of trees were used for specific forms of magic, and the wands and staffs found among archeological discoveries from this time period are typically made of iron and bronze. However, wooden staffs have also been discovered in the graves of seeresses. As with the Druids, we can assume that wooden wands were in wide use among the Norse magicians, but the evidence has decayed over the centuries.

Like the Irish and their Ogham, the ancient Germanics also had a system for writing that was related both to magic and to trees. The first Germanic alphabet, known as the Elder Futhark, was developed sometime around the first century CE, and several newer alphabets evolved from the Elder Futhark over time, as the Germanic languages diversified due to widespread migration.

The symbols that made up these various related alphabets are known collectively as the runes. While some of these symbols were adapted from other nearby cultures (most likely in northern Italy) many had already existed as powerful magical symbols among the Germanic tribes. These symbols had been used in magical workings, possibly for thousands of years. By carving the symbols into objects made from stone, bone, metal, and—of course—wood, a rune master could change the course of unfolding events.

Several rune names in these symbolic systems correspond to specific sacred trees. For example, the rune called Ansuz, in the Elder Futhark system, is associated with the ash tree. Another rune, Eihwaz, literally translates to "yew." Berkana is translated both as "birch tree" and "birch goddess." In the Anglo-Saxon rune system, Ansuz evolved into the runes Asec, meaning "ash," and Ac, which translates to "oak tree." The rune Yr stands for a bow made from the branch of a Yew tree.

The magical energies of these trees were part of what imbued these specific symbols with their power. Even the word "rune" is associated with a magical tree—the Old Norse word *runa* is the root word for "rowan," which is sacred to both the Celts and the Norse, and is known in some places as "the rune tree."

Runes were also used in divination, according to the ancient writer Tacitus. The diviners would harvest a branch from a fruit-bearing tree, cut it into strips, and carve a symbol on each one. A white cloth was laid upon the ground, and the carved strips of wood were scattered upon it. The rune reader would look up toward the sky to ask the gods for their assistance before choosing three of the symbols at random. These three were then interpreted for information about the question being asked.

Runic symbols are still used in modern forms of magic and divination today by modern practitioners of reconstructed Norse traditions, such as Asatru and Heathenism, as well as by some eclectic Wiccans and other Witches. The runes' individual meanings and divinatory interpretations are derived both from historical sources and intuitive associations.

For example, Ansuz (ash), named for the tree on which Odin is said to have hung in order to obtain the secrets of the runes, is often interpreted to indicate messages from the higher realms. Ansuz is used in magic today to gain wisdom in confusing situations and to communicate with the divine. Eiwhaz (yew) is associated with death and regeneration. In magic, this rune is a strong symbol of protection, banishing, and spiritual development. Berkana (birch) signifies new beginnings and growth. It is used in magic for fertility, creativity, and strengthening family ties.

One of the better-known Germanic magical practices is the creation of a runic talisman, by carving runes appropriate to the purpose into a piece of wood or other natural material. Traditionally, this "tine," as it is called, is made from a branch harvested from a live tree, after securing the tree's permission.

Tree-related customs handed down from the Germanic peoples exist elsewhere in Europe and beyond, in both Pagan and Christian contexts. The maypole, a central feature of May Day and Beltane celebrations, is believed to be a remnant of the earliest Germanic tribal rituals, which would have focused on a living tree, as opposed to a cut pole.

And the Christmas tree, of course, is an adaptation of the Yule celebrations of old. It is believed that church missionaries in the Early Middle Ages essentially coopted the beliefs and rituals of the local people by bringing their traditional object of worship—the evergreen tree—into the celebration of the newly imposed holiday instead.

Despite the Church's best efforts, however, trees have remained mystical, magical, and sacred to many modern-day descendants of the ancient Germans.

TREES IN
WICCAN COSMOLOGY

When compared to the religious traditions of the Celts and the ancient Germans, the central tenets and practices of Traditional Wicca are not quite as heavily focused on trees.

The origins of what we now call Wicca, as developed by Gerald Gardner and others in the mid-twentieth century, seem to have largely emphasized worship of the Goddess and God, the celebration of fertility, and the natural cycles of life and death. And in terms of ritual practice, Gardner was more influenced by medieval occult texts and ceremonial magic than by the remnants of Druidic or Germanic lore and customs that may have still existed where he lived.

That being said, Gardner's first real experiences with what he referred to as Witchcraft took place in the area of England known as New Forest, which was also the name of the coven he is said to have been initiated into, and he named his own coven "Bricket Wood." Both of these were already names of places, of course, but they nonetheless carried an acknowledgment of the sacred quality of the forest.

When it comes to Wiccan cosmology, trees are obviously a part of Nature, and therefore they are part of the realm of the Goddess and the God. One of the chief archetypes in Wiccan deity is the God of the Forest, also known as the God of the Hunt, so trees certainly have a place of importance in the traditional Wiccan worldview. Additional archetypes worshipped in some Wiccan traditions include the Oak King and the Holly King, and the Green Man (or Green Woman). Furthermore, trees are intricately connected with the Wheel of the Year, and can be seen as excellent representatives of the Elements.

Next, we'll take a closer look at these important components of modern Wicca.

THE OAK KING
AND THE HOLLY KING

One way in which trees show up in some Wiccan traditions, specifically, is in the legend of the Oak King and the Holly King. Said to be Celtic in origin, the tale presents the Oak King as the ruler of summer and the light half of the year, while the Holly King rules winter and the dark half.

The eternal turning of the two halves of the year is represented by a battle between the two kings, who are seen as rivaling brothers, each fighting for dominance and taking turns conquering the other. In some versions of the legend, the winning king actually kills the other, but each is always reborn, to rise and grow in strength until he reigns again.

These two trees were particularly significant to the Druids, who met for rituals in oak groves and used holly for decorating at the Winter Solstice. Their somewhat similar-looking leaves, their coexistence in northern forests, and their considerable differences make them rather appropriate for a legend about sibling rivals who take turns reigning over the world.

In the summer months, oak trees make a mighty impression with their tall height and far-reaching branches thick with elegantly shaped leaves. Holly, by contrast, is generally quite short, and blends in with the greenery of all the other low-growing trees. Once all the deciduous trees have dropped their leaves, however, the bright, shining leaves of the holly remain to get all the attention, and the red berries they produce in the cold season provides extra cheer.

Introduced into modern Paganism by Robert Graves via *The White Goddess*, and later incorporated into Wiccan practice by Janet and Stewart Farrar, the Oak King and Holly King have been adapted by some as aspects of the God, in addition to his more traditional aspects of the Sun and the Horned God of the forest. However, for many others, the tale is seen simply as a metaphor for the sometimes-fierce back-and-forth dance between the seasons as the Wheel of the Year continues to turn.

The battles between the two kings are often reenacted in group rituals at the appropriate Sabbats. In some versions of the legend, the Oak King wins the battle at the Spring Equinox, or Ostara, when the balance of light and dark officially tips toward the Summer Solstice. The Holly King then takes over at the Autumnal Equinox, or Mabon, when the balance tips back toward winter. In other traditions, the battles and resulting change in power occur at the Solstices themselves—Litha and Yule. But no matter which calendar is followed, this story of the ongoing tug-of-war between the two brothers is often used to illustrate the nature of duality—light cannot exist without the dark, as life cannot exist without death.

In centuries past, before the benefit of artificial lighting, the difference between the "dark" and "light" halves of the year would certainly have been more stark than what we experience today, with much more in the way of real-life consequences for the people. Viewed this way, it makes sense that the turning of the seasons might be viewed in the harsh terms of battle, victory, and death—especially in cultures accustomed to skirmishes and wars in the first place.

In the 21st century, however, some contemporary Wiccans aren't crazy about the "fight" aspect of the legend, pointing out that in their native habitat, the trees are no threat to each other, and that in any case the prevailing cosmology of Wicca isn't about conflict or competition, but rather cooperation and harmony between all aspects of nature. So some choose to observe the Oak and Holly kings as mere representatives of the seasons, each stepping forth into the spotlight and back again according to their nature. Others leave the legend out of their practice altogether.

THE GREEN MAN
(AND GREEN WOMAN)

Another tree-related archetype that some Wiccans incorporate into their practice is the "Green Man." Arguably older and much more widespread than the legend of the Oak King and Holly King, the Green Man is an ancient symbol that has been carved into churches, cathedrals, and other public buildings since at least the days of ancient Rome, but the image is theorized to be even older.

There are many variations of the symbol, but typically the Green Man is presented as a face either composed of or surrounded by leaves and vines, as if he is hiding in the forest and just barely visible. In some versions, he has vines or branches coming out of his mouth, ears, nose, and/or eyes as well. In several cases he has a body as well as a head, though the face alone is what we typically think of when it comes to the Green Man.

He is often cited as being a Celtic symbol, and has been connected specifically with the god Cernunnos. But while he is found throughout Celtic Europe (though predominantly in Britain and France), he also appears in parts of India and the Middle East. So it would seem that our Western version of this archetype may have grown out of something older and more universal.

In any case, the Green Man got his English name only in the early-mid 20th century, when British folklorist Lady Raglan connected these symbols on English churches to the "Jack of the Green," a mythical figure in English folk traditions. This figure symbolized the fertility and new growth of the spring season, and was often part of May Day (Beltane) celebrations, represented by a man wearing a very tall costume made of leaves.

While most of the Green Man carvings around the world do seem to depict a male face, many observers have noted the presence of a Green Woman in more than a few instances. In some images, the Green Woman is giving birth to the leaves and vines, and as such has been connected to the Sheela-na-gig, a naked female figure believed to symbolize both fertility and protection from the evil eye. (The classic

Sheela-na-gig image is found most commonly in Ireland, and does not typically include tree imagery. Nonetheless, a few exceptions do exist, tying these two mysterious archetypes together.)

Many hold that the Green Man (or Green Woman) represents the spiritual presence one often feels when walking through a forest. It's as if some unseen sentient being is watching as we make our way along a path, or stop to observe the sounds of birds and other animals. As the trees begin to leaf out in the spring, becoming fully lush during the summer, they hide much from view, filling in the empty spaces that had been left by the winter months of bare branches. In this sense, the Green Man can be said to represent the divinity hidden within plain sight that such greenery often evokes.

In some traditions of Wicca, the Green Man is seen as an aspect of the God, in addition to his aspects of the Sun God and the Horned God of the forest. This aspect is celebrated specifically during the warm-weather Sabbats, starting with Beltane in May and in some cases going all the way through to Mabon, the Autumn Equinox.

There is not an exact female equivalent, in the sense of the Green Woman as an aspect of the Goddess, but a parallel can be drawn nonetheless to the Mother Earth aspect of the female deity. At any rate, whether we consider the male or female version of the Green figure, or both, the imagery is a fitting one to associate with Wicca and Witchcraft at large.

THE WHEEL AND THE ELEMENTS

Aside from these somewhat eclectic archetypes (or, for some, aspects of deity), there is much about trees themselves that make them emblematic of the spirit and natural focus of Wicca. Deciduous trees, for starters, are especially perfect embodiments of the cycles of the seasons in their own right, serving as pivotal markers on the Wheel of the Year.

Trees provide us with some of the first signs of spring, as subtle, velvety buds begin to emerge at the tips of otherwise-bare branches.

As the weather warms, the buds begin to open as blossoms and the tiniest starts of the leaves push through into the light.

Leaves continue to grow as the days lengthen, with most trees in full leaf by early summer. Like the agricultural societies who gave us much of our Pagan lore and tradition, the trees themselves are busy all summer long, capturing the energy of the Sun and converting it into the food they need to continue living through the dark, winter months.

As the daylight wanes and autumn grows nearer, some of the first leaves will begin to turn and fall from the trees. Like our ancestors, they are preparing for winter now in earnest, producing fruits to ensure the future survival of their species, as well as the buds that their new leaves will grow from when the strong Sun returns.

Soon, all the leaves will fall from their perches, but not before blazing with the colors of the Sun as a final salute before the annual "death" of the light. Once all the branches are bare and stark against greying skies, we know that the dormant winter season is upon us. It will be a few long months before the trees signal to us again that the light and warmth are making their return.

Trees, like other plant life, are also ultimate embodiments of the Elements in action. In addition to being homes for nymphs, fairies, and other Elemental beings, they represent each of the Elemental forces in unique ways. Trees are solid and literally rooted in the soil. They require at least some amount of water to survive. Trees that grow near creeks and rivers help to keep them from overflowing their banks, as their roots keep the soil in place. In this way they participate in the relationship between the Element of Water and the Element of Earth.

Trees work with the air in the form of breezes which carry their seeds to new locations, ensuring the reproduction of their species. Their blowing branches can also warn us of coming winds and storms. Trees also co-create with the Element of Fire, as their growth is spurred by sunlight and they literally transform the energy of light into nutritional substance. And the destructive force of a forest fire clears out overgrown floor cover that can choke out new life, in order to allow the forest as a whole to continue to thrive.

Of course, like everything else on the Earth plane, trees are suffused with the Fifth Element—Spirit, or Akasha, the unifying Element that is present in every particle of the Universe. But there is also just something about a grove of trees—a sense of mystery, of "otherworldliness," a distinct energy that commands our attention and reverence. Whether we understand this energy as the presence of individual spirits, fairies, or aspects of deity, or even something less defined, there's no denying that trees truly embody the Element of Spirit.

Clearly, trees are inextricably interconnected with all of Nature, and therefore so is tree magic. We can see this easily through the lens of the Elements and the energies that each can lend to our magic when called upon.

Tree magic can be worked with the Element of Air simply by watching leaves flutter in the wind and observing images and messages that come through in their dance. The Element of Earth can be honored in the ritual planting of new trees, and in any spells that involve burying a charm made from bark, leaves, nuts, fruits, and/or blossoms.

Spells and rituals that call for setting energy-infused leaves or bark to float on streams, rivers, lakes or oceans are drawing on the Element of Water. And the Element of Fire, of course, is present for every ritual fire and any candle spell incorporating tree ingredients.

TREES AND
TOOLS OF THE CRAFT

In addition to the roles trees play in Wiccan beliefs and philosophies, they also provide the raw materials for important components of Craft practice. Many an old tree stump has been used as an altar for outdoor rituals, and groves are still a beloved place to worship the God and Goddess.

When it comes to ritual tools, there are three powerful tree-based treasures still in use today that can be traced back through our ancestral lineage for millennia: the wand (or stave), the broom (or besom), and the bonfire (or balefire).

THE WAND

In Wicca and many other forms modern Paganism, the wand is a sacred tool. Depending on the tradition one follows (or one's individual eclectic practice), the wand may be used in ritual, spellwork (especially in ceremonial magic), meditation, and/or astral journeying.

The wand has a long history, going back at least as far as the Zoroastrian religion of the 6th century BCE, when priests used a barsom—a bundle of twigs—to establish a link between the material and spiritual realms. A similar bundle was used by the ancient fire priests ("flamines") of Rome. As we saw earlier, the Druids of the ancient Celts and and the Norse seeresses also used wands for magic. Wands also appear in ancient Greek myth, as well as in records of magic spells from Egypt. These ancient societies in turn influenced the practices of medieval magicians, who included much lore and instruction regarding wands in their magical texts, known as grimoires.

But the wand is not just a tool of European origin. Shamanic traditions from Africa to Asia to South America have employed wands in a variety of ways. Actually, the wand is only one type of a broader category of magical tools made from trees, known as "staves." A stave can be a wand, a staff, a stang (a forked staff) or other rod-shaped tool.

The staff, a much longer and quite possibly much older version of the wand, has been a symbol of power and leadership in many different religions around the world, including Christianity. It was held during ritual and carried during travel by shamans, magicians, and healers alike. Among our pagan ancestors, the staff was used for protective magic, directing energy, and invoking spiritual entities, among other things.

Like the wand, the staff is mentioned plenty in medieval grimoires, and the two tools are considered to have the same magical powers and uses. The chief difference between them is size—a staff is typically long enough to be used as a walking stick, while a wand is usually no longer than a foot or so, and is often tapered at one end.

While the staff is less prevalent than the wand in Wiccan practice, it is incorporated into some forms of Wicca, as well as many other traditions within the wider world of modern Witchcraft. For the sake of simplicity, this guide will focus only on the wand, but if you would like to work with a staff instead, or with both, then by all means do so!

With some notable exceptions, such as the bronze staffs of the Norse volur mentioned above, and the metal and ivory wands of the ancient Egyptians, the wands of our pagan ancestors were typically made from the branches of trees. This choice was not simply down to whether other materials were available—in fact, wood was still the preferred option for many practitioners. For while we know that metal is a conductor of electricity, wood is actually a means through which other kinds of energy can be transmitted.

We've already seen that trees were considered by the ancients to be a link between the physical and spiritual realms. It follows then that the branches of trees could serve this function as well, in a manner that allowed the wand's user to specifically direct the energy of this connection.

In some traditions, particularly those inspired by the ancient Celts, it is the spirit of the tree the wand is made from that facilitates the magical action being performed. The wand becomes an extension of the spiritual energy of the individual tree, as well as the archetypal spirit of the species of tree it was made from. Therefore, a wand made from an oak branch will have different energetic properties than a wand made from the branch of a hazel or rowan tree.

However, as with any magical tool, a wand in and of itself has no real power. It is the joining of the will, or intent, of the magician with the energetic capacities of the wand that makes magic happen. Some say that the wand is a representation of the magician's will, which is ultimately true, but the same can be said of other magical tools, as well as spell ingredients.

It may be more accurate in this case to say that the wand is used to focus and direct the energy of the intention, or will, of its user. Its linear shape enables a clear visualization of both the energy itself and the destination to which it is sent. It can almost be compared to a pointer used by a presenter in a lecture hall, only the lecturer is you, and the audience is the spiritual entities you are working with, whether they be Elemental beings, specific deities, or simply the energies of the Universe in general.

Wands are used for a variety of purposes in Wiccan and other contemporary Pagan ritual and magic. On the altar, the wand can be used to represent the God, as well as the Element of Fire or Air, depending on the tradition. The wand and athame serve similar functions, and may be used interchangeably for certain aspects of ritual. In ceremonial-inspired magic, the wand is used to tap or point to specific components (or ingredients) of a spell, infusing them with magical energy, and to draw runes and other magical symbols in the air over the work. They can also be used to send the cumulative energy of the spell in a specific direction, known in some circles as "blasting."

Wands have also been used to invoke spirits as well as to send them back to where they came from. In their traditional shamanic capacity, wands can serve to open the "doors" between the material and spiritual realms, facilitating safe astral travel. Wands have also been used as divining tools, or "dowsers," helping to find underground sources of water and other secrets hidden under the Earth, such as ancient burial sites.

The art of wand-making is a tradition in and of itself, and the old grimoires are full of various instructions and specifications for doing so. The *Key of Solomon*, for example, recommends elder and hazel as ideal wand wood, and Wednesday at sunrise as the best time for harvesting the branch. Various sources recommend different lengths, widths, and materials, as well as rituals for consecrating the newly-made wand.

It is ideal, ultimately, to make your own wand, because then it is infused from the beginning with your own unique personal energy. But of course, this isn't strictly necessary, and if you feel drawn to purchase a wand made by another, then that is the best wand for you at this point on your personal path. If you do want to make your own tree-sourced wand, however, you'll find some suggestions for doing so in Part Three of this guide.

THE BROOM

The broom, of course, remains a hallmark image of the stereotypical fantasy "witch" in mainstream culture, serving as a literal vehicle for those with the magical know-how to soar into the night sky. Actual Witches know that what "flying" really means is astral travel, which can be achieved with (or without) the assistance of certain psychotropic plants. Recipes for "flying ointments" are found in sources dating back to ancient times. (However, many of these contained toxic ingredients, and it is not recommended to try them yourself!)

The origins of the association between broomsticks and flying may be related to the use of flying ointments, but a more likely source is an old pagan fertility ritual that involved "riding" astride broomsticks, pitchforks, and other pole-shaped objects through agricultural fields, while jumping high into the air to encourage crops to grow.

At any rate, many long-standing pagan traditions have incorporated the humble broom. In handfasting customs in Wales, the newlyweds would jump over a broomstick together for fertility. The Celts were said to associate the broom with the fairy realm. Some legends told of Witches who sought the fairies' assistance in finding the perfect branch in the forest for making a magical broom.

Brooms were used to clear out negative energy from the home, and to prepare a household energetically for the birth of a child. They were also placed upright near the door of the home, or hung horizontally above the door, for protection.

Traditionally, a broom for use in magic, known as a besom, was made with a handle of hazel, ash, or oak, and bristles made from birch twigs. Thin strips of willow wood held the bristles to the handle. It is said that a few ancient besoms have been found with secret compartments inside the handle which held herbs, oils, and other potential spell ingredients. Whether or not this is the case, it's easy to see how a seemingly "common" household implement could help Witches disguise their Craft during the perilous witch-hunts of the Middle Ages.

Today, sacred brooms are still placed against or near doors to protect the home from unwanted visitors (both from the Earth plane and from the spiritual realm). They are also used to ritually sweep out stale or negative energy from indoor environments, and to prepare sacred space before ritual. (Typically, the bristles of a sacred broom never touch the floor—the "sweeping" is more symbolic, but still serves its energetic purpose.) Some Wiccans use a besom to close the circle at the end of ritual, dispersing any leftover energies, but beyond these purposes it is not typically considered a core ritual tool.

In many Craft traditions, the broom is associated with the element of Water, due to its purifying function, and is sacred to the Goddess. However, other traditions view the broom as evenly balanced between the genders, with the handle representing the divine masculine, and the bristles the divine feminine.

Like the wand, the broom can be made from wood chosen for its particular magical energies. But unlike the wand, the broom also has a mundane purpose, and therefore can be a magical tool hidden in plain sight within the home, which works well for Witches who aren't "out of the broom closet" and practice in complete secrecy. Whether it's a common household broom or the small, decorative kind, your "besom in disguise" can still be used to guard your door, and no one will be the wiser.

A regular household broom can be a handy alternative to harvesting twigs and branches to make your own, or buying a special besom in a magical supply shop. You can simply charge a normal broom—preferably one with a wooden handle—to use for ritual purposes. Just make sure it's a brand new broom, and that you don't use it for regular household cleaning. Or, if you prefer, you can just use a tree branch—preferably one with smaller, twig-sized branches still attached—as a symbolic "broom" for the ritual sweeping of a space.

THE BONFIRE

There can be no fire without fuel, and trees have long provided fuel for the fires that have kept us warm and nourished since humans first discovered it. Many Wiccan and other Pagan traditions celebrate the Sabbats with a ritual bonfire, especially Beltane, Litha, and Samhain. These fires are known as "bale fires" in Celtic-influenced traditions, a term stemming from the ancient fire festival of Beltane in early Ireland.

Falling at the beginning of May, the traditional start to summer in the Celtic world, Beltane honored the ancient Sun god Bel. The smoke from the sacred Beltane fires was used to purify the community's cattle and crops for the season, and embers from the central "Bel-fire" (or *Bealteine*, in Irish Gaelic) were used to relight hearth fires throughout the land. Of course, many other ancient European pagan cultures held ritual and celebratory fires as well, including the Greeks, Romans, and Norse.

Many forms of Wicca observe a tradition of "nine sacred woods," a list of nine different types of trees whose wood is considered the most magical for burning in a ritual fire. Special fires, such as those at

Beltane, might be comprised of all nine, though since this is often not practical, a combination of two or more may be used. Like the bale fire itself, this tradition also traces back to Celtic lore, where several references to nine sacred (or "blessed") trees can be found among mythology, poetry, and song.

The types of trees vary from source to source, but most include oak, rowan, willow, hawthorn, and hazel. Other trees named in some sources, but not others, include ash, holly, apple, elm, and alder. Ultimately, the differences among the Celtic references might depend simply upon location, as it would be most practical to use whatever wood could be found near one's home.

The modern poem known as the Wiccan Rede includes a mention of "nine woods," which are birch, oak, rowan, willow, hawthorn, hazel, apple, fir, and elder. These nine are viewed by some Wiccans as the appropriate "sacred woods" for ritual fires. However, it's unclear whether this part of the Rede is a direct reference to the ancient tradition of the bale fire, since it's the "cauldron" into which the woods are said to go, and the last line of this passage warns against burning elder, lest one be cursed. (Elder is strongly associated with witches and death in medieval lore, and also makes very poor firewood, which may explain this particular warning.)

Another potential source for selecting the appropriate nine trees is the Celtic tree calendar described earlier. The first nine trees of the calendar are birch, rowan, ash, alder, willow, hawthorn, oak, holly, and hazel.

Along with the special Sabbat fires, covens as well as solitary Witches may honor the Full Moon with a ritual bonfire, choosing wood that fits the ritual theme or magical goal(s) of the gathering.

If you're fortunate enough to have a working fireplace in your home, you can also integrate this practice into your magic, by burning purpose-appropriate wood in the hearth during ritual and/or spellwork. For example, you might burn oak in the fireplace while working spells for healing or prosperity, and apple or maple for love magic.

If you choose to incorporate ritual fire into your practice, be sure to acquire your firewood in the most ecologically responsible way possible. When purchasing, look for wood from certified-sustainable sources so you're not supporting reckless deforestation. If you're out foraging for your bonfire, leave hollow logs alone, as they provide homes for woodland animals.

Whenever possible, source your firewood from fallen trees and consider using recycled wood fuel in lieu of virgin wood in your home hearth. These are good ways to respect the spiritual energies of the tree kingdom, and the Earth as a whole, while still enjoying an age-old magical tradition.

AT THE FOREST'S EDGE

As we have seen, trees have been with us both physically and spiritually since the earliest days of human existence. Modern Wiccan and other Pagan traditions echo the reverence our ancestors held for these magnificent beings. But while working magic with a wooden wand or clearing space with a besom of twigs does connect us to the energy of trees, nothing beats interacting with the physical presence of an actual living tree, whether you're in a magnificent forest or just in your own back yard.

Part Two offers suggestions for connecting deliberately with whatever trees you have access to in your physical world. You'll also meet 13 trees with long-standing magical reputations, and discover their individual properties and uses. So get ready to start developing your own unique practice of tree magic!

PART TWO

WORKING MAGIC
WITH TREES

CONNECTING WITH LIVING, MAGICAL BEINGS

Wiccans and other Witches are typically among the most ardent nature-lovers you can find. However, that doesn't mean we're all avid hikers or well-versed in botany. There are plenty of Witches who work regularly with dried herbs from magical supply shops, yet wouldn't be able to recognize the plants they come from if their lives depended on it.

This shouldn't be considered a failing—in fact, it's one of the perks of the 21st-century that we have such easy access to magical ingredients from all over the world. However, taking your practice further by learning all you can about your magical allies—in this case, the trees—is immensely rewarding.

To that end, Part Two will introduce you to the history, lore, and unique characteristics of 13 of the most commonly used trees in magic. You'll also find tips for forming more intentional personal connections with trees, and opening up to the magical wisdom they have to offer.

GETTING UP
CLOSE AND PERSONAL

Most forms of tree magic don't require you to be in the physical presence of an actual tree. For example, ritual and spellwork often involve the use of a tree's bark, branches, leaves, and/or flowers, which can be used indoors at your altar. And you can find tree-based incense, bark, and essential oils in magical supply shops and online, which may come from just about anywhere on the planet. So you don't need to live anywhere near a cedar tree, for example, to benefit from the magical energies of its aromatic essence.

Furthermore, trees can be represented visually in your magical space, whether through sketches or photographs, or more abstract or symbolic artwork. And, as we will see in Part Three, you can connect to the spiritual energy of a tree or even a whole forest through focused visualization. So if you live in a community or region where trees are scarce, your practice of tree magic can still be rich and varied if you take advantage of these methods.

That being said, it is extremely beneficial (and highly advised) to spend at least a little time with one or more actual, live trees, to the extent that this is possible for you. If you're blessed with a yard that contains a tree or two, this is a great place to start. Otherwise, find a park, a greenway, or some other place where you can have direct access to at least one tree.

Ideally, you'll be able to place your hands on the tree's trunk, and/or sit in its shade. (You can bring a blanket to sit on and even make it a picnic!) If you live anywhere near a forest with hiking trails, make a point of treating yourself to a hike every once in awhile—even if it's just a short, easy walk.

Get in the habit of observing the trees you pass on your way from place to place in your daily life, whether they're grand evergreens along the highway or small ornamental maples outside a shopping center. Gently brush a leaf with your hand as you walk under a tree on the sidewalk, and give it a silent greeting. In the winter, take time to appreciate the shapes made by the bare branches of deciduous trees. Too often, trees just blend into the artificial landscape of our modern world. Make a point of noticing them for what they are—living, magical beings.

A wonderful way to gain a deeper understanding of the magical energy of trees is to return to the same tree, grove, or forest at least once during every season. Bring a camera and take pictures so that you can document the changes the trees go through over the course of the year. Ideally, continue to visit the same tree(s) as often as possible, as this is a great way to establish an energetic relationship with a single tree or grove. Just as you need to work with your ritual and magical tools over time in order to deepen your connection to them, you can enhance your connection with trees that are special to you by communing with them regularly.

As you develop your awareness of trees in your environment, you will likely begin picking up on their ethereal energies, and may even notice how they interact with the spiritual plane. Gaze at the trunk or the canopy of a tree with a soft focus, and watch for faces to appear in the bark, leaves, or branches. Look also at the negative spaces around and between branches, as sometimes images appear in the dance between the canopy and the surrounding sky. Windy days are great for this form of scrying, as the leaves and branches may form moving pictures.

In fact, wind itself is another method through which the Universe can communicate with you via trees. Have you ever watched a tree and noticed just two or three leaves fluttering in a breeze while the rest of the tree is still? Those micro currents of air are not merely air but gentle signals from the magical living energy of the tree itself. And if you're having an introspective moment near a tree and a sudden gust of wind shakes the leaves, consider what your most recent thought was—you might be getting confirmation of an idea or insight!

IDENTIFYING AND HARVESTING FROM TREES

If you're just beginning to work magically with trees, you might be totally lost when it comes to recognizing the type of tree you're looking for. Don't feel bad—most of us have never been taught much, if anything, about plant identification!

Happily, there's plenty of information out there on identifying trees based on the shape of their leaves, the appearance of their trunks and branches, and other characteristics. You can also find help with distinguishing between types of trees that look quite similar, such as the many different kinds of conifers.

Online sources are a great place to start, but you might also want to have a physical copy of a good field guide to trees in your area. You'll find a few suggestions in the recommended reading list at the end of this book.

Another great way to learn tree identification is to visit a botanical garden or arboretum where trees are labeled by species, or a local tree nursery where experts can introduce you to trees you might be unfamiliar with.

Once you've found a tree you'd like to utilize in a spell or ritual, you'll need to consider how best to harvest the bark, branches, leaves, berries, and/or flowers that the magical working calls for. There are a variety of methods for taking a part of a tree in a respectful manner, and all begin with asking for and receiving permission from the spirit of the tree.

This tradition goes back to the days of the ancient pagans, but some Witches today prefer to avoid harvesting anything from a living tree, and instead gather only what the tree has already shed on the ground. This is a personal choice that only you can make, and will depend on what your intuition tells you.

If you do choose to harvest from a live tree, you'll need to research how best to go about it while doing minimal damage to the tree. You'll find more on this topic, including a suggested ritual for respectful harvesting, in Part Three.

THIRTEEN
MAGICAL TREES

The trees featured here have been regarded as magical and/or sacred by cultures in both North America and ancient Europe. (One exception is maple, which evidently was not considered an important magical tree in the Old World, but which is highly valued by the descendants of native North Americans and immigrants alike.)

Because Wicca and other forms of the Craft came to the U.S. and Canada via Europe, the history and lore, medicinal uses, and magical uses and associations are on the whole derived from European rather than Native American traditions, with the exception of a few brief details.

The descriptions in this section are largely generalized to the common name for each tree, rather than individual species, which often have their own more specified magical uses and associations. You can apply the information here to any species of the tree, and/or do some research into each individual species for even more information.

For example, if you live in the desert, you can work with emory oak the same way you'd work with white oak in the Midwest. But you can also look into magical aspects of emory oak that may differ from those of white oak, and tweak your spellwork accordingly.

Depending on where you live, some or many of these trees may not be native to your area. However, every geographic region within the continental U.S. and Canada is represented by at least a couple of trees on this list. In addition, be aware that the lists of example species for each tree are by no means exhaustive, so it's well worth doing your own research to see what additional species might grow in your area.

Finally, you may find plenty of cultivated trees, in yards, parks, and other public areas, that are not native to North America but rather imported from Europe, Asia, or elsewhere. While this guide focuses on native trees, it really doesn't matter in the slightest to your magic, so work with whatever trees are near you!

Finally, a cautionary note: the medical uses described here are for information purposes only, and are not intended to serve as instructional, nor should they be used in place of needed medical care by a physician. If you decide to experiment with any part of any tree for healing purposes, be sure to research thoroughly and know that in this context, the particular species of tree is *very* important to identify, as not all species will have the same physiological effects on the human body.

Note – larger versions of the illustrations featured in this section are available at www.wiccaliving.com/trees

ASH
(FRAXINUS SPP)

<u>Common North American species:</u> black ash, blue ash, Carolina ash, green ash, Oregon ash, singleleaf ash, white ash

<u>Range of native habitat:</u> all regions of continental U.S.; Eastern and Western Canada

The ash genus consists of roughly 65 species, most of which reach between 40 and 60 feet in height at maturity. Technically, the ash "leaf" is a set of individual "leaflets" which grow in pairs directly opposite each other on the stem, with a single leaflet at the end.

Ash has strong, thick twigs and a large, deep root system. Some species are threatened by an invasive beetle called the emerald ash borer, which feeds on the bark of native ash. Ash is sometimes confused with mountain ash, which is a common name in North America for rowan trees, but they are not related.

Among our pagan ancestors, the ash was a highly significant tree. In origin stories from both ancient Greece and Scandinavia, the first human man was created from an ash tree. The Celts viewed the ash as the connector of the three interlinking circles of existence—past, present, and future—and it is one of the fairy triad of trees (along with oak and hawthorn). Druids made wands and magical charms from ash wood, and it has long served as the wood for the handle of the besom, or ritual broom, in traditional Witchcraft.

Ash was seen as having protective and healing properties, particularly when it came to children. In Ireland, an energy healer (or "fairy doctor") would often hold a wand of ash during ritual prayer. In Britain, a small amount of ash sap was fed to newborn babies to keep them healthy. Ill or injured children were brought to a young ash or sapling and passed naked through a cleft cut into the tree, which was then bound together to heal as the child healed. In some places it was believed that the tree and the child were connected for life, so the tree was watched over and often studded with nails to prevent it from being cut down for its wood.

Ash was a traditional wood for the Yule log, and, as we saw in Part One, has long been thought to be the Yggdrasil, or World Tree, of Norse cosmology. Although it is now believed by scholars that this was not the case, the association is widespread and longstanding enough that any energetic association one feels with the ash in this context is perfectly valid. Either way, it is still known as a tree of enchantment, of timelessness, of existing between and across the visible and invisible worlds.

Ash bark has astringent and diuretic properties, and has been used in infusions to treat liver and intestinal issues, rheumatism, and malaria. It also works to reduce fevers and soothe sore throats, and to treat kidney and urinary infections. A tea made from the leaves of European ash was used to treat jaundice, rheumatism, and gout. Ash tree and flower essences aid with self-knowledge and trusting in one's own authority.

Magically, ash is used for protection (especially during travel on or near water), prosperity, healing, wisdom, and spiritual growth. Ash connects us to the unseen realms and the liminal spaces outside linear time, and so is particularly good for prophetic dreaming. Place fresh ash leaves under your pillow for more clear and enhanced dreams, and be sure to write down anything of significance the next morning. As the connecting point between past, present, and future, it puts us in touch with the energy of creation, making it an excellent ally in workings related to creativity (especially the literary arts).

For protection from illness, place a few fresh ash leaves in a bowl of blessed water near your bed before going to sleep. The bark can also be added to witch jars and poppets for protection. For prosperity, burn a log of ash at Yule, or use ash bark as loose incense. Make charms for healing, love, or prosperity out of small ash twigs and carry them with you until your desire has manifested. Ash wood is a good conductor of energy and makes excellent wands, particularly for the purpose of astral travel and healing, but also for workings related to personal transformation, balance, harmony, and rain magic.

Magical Associations:

Gender: Masculine, Feminine
Element: Fire, Air, Water
Planet: Sun, Neptune
Zodiac: Pisces, Aries

<u>Deities:</u> Poseidon, Jupiter, Mars, Minerva, Odin, Thor, Frigg, Lir, Manannan

BIRCH
(BETULA SPP)

<u>Common North American species:</u> paper birch, river birch, sweet birch, yellow birch

<u>Range of native habitat:</u> Northeastern, Midwestern, parts of Southern U.S., Appalachia, Alaska; Eastern, Western, and Northern Canada

A slender yet deceptively hardy tree, birch is most often associated with the bright white bark of the paper birch species. In fact, the etymology of "birch" can be traced back to Indo-European words related to "brilliance, brightness, shimmer, and glitter" in various contemporary languages.

Birches have double-toothed, slightly heart-shaped leaves and can grow to heights of 50 to 70 feet. One of the first trees to flower in the spring, birch is also one of the first to naturally establish after a forest has been cleared, and was one of the first to emerge after the last ice age. Hence, birch has long been seen as a symbol of new beginnings.

In ancient Northern Europe, birch was widely seen as a protective tree, especially of women and children. Twigs and branches were brought into the home for protection, and cradles were made from the wood to keep malevolent fairies away from the child. Carrying a piece of birch was thought to protect against kidnapping by the fairies. In Scandinavia, birch trees were planted in front of the home to protect all within the household. In Ireland, people carried amulets of birch branches marked with Ogham inscriptions.

For the Celts, birch was also a tree of purification, used to drive out the "spirits of the old year" from the home, and the traditional besom, or ritual broom, was made of birch twigs. Fertility, love, and marriage were widely associated with birch. Birch twigs were used to light the Beltane fires, and could be used to grant fertility to a barren cow.

In the Gaulish region of Europe, birch twigs were lit during marriage ceremonies for fertility and luck. In Wales, birch branches were woven into wreaths and given as love tokens. Birch was sometimes used as the maypole tree for May Day celebrations, and couples in Scandinavia would frolic in birch to celebrate the beginning of summer. The Norse rune Berkana translates to "birch tree" or "birch goddess" and symbolizes matters related to birth and motherhood.

Birch bark has been used medicinally for treating muscle soreness, burns and wounds, and other skin conditions such as eczema. Birch bark essential oil has also been used as an insect repellent. The leaves are used in a tea to treat rheumatism and gout, dissolve kidney stones, and to heal sores in the mouth. A yellow fungus known as chaga mushrooms that grows on the trunks of birches has long been used by Native Americans to treat tumors, and is now gaining notoriety both for treatment and prevention of cancer.

Magically, birch is a symbol of birth, renewal, purification, and fresh starts. It is highly powerful when used in magic worked at the New Moon, for beginning new projects, for channeling divine feminine energy, and for love, beauty, and protection. Carry birch twigs or bark in a protection charm, particularly against negative energy or psychic attack. Use a besom made with birch to purify the energy of your home at the New Year, either right after Samhain or Yule, depending on your tradition.

Birch is also known as a tree of illumination, because of how well birch bark can be seen at night in a forest, especially in moonlight. This makes birch ideal for shadow work, when you need to see aspects of your inner self that are blocked and therefore holding you back from making progress in an area of your life. The tree essence is used to "peel" away old layers of self in order to allow your true self to shine through.

It is also excellent for workings related to renewing energy after illness or other difficult circumstances. To release energies from a past situation, write a word or phrase representing the issue on a piece of birch bark and set it afloat on a river or stream.

Magical Associations:

Gender: Feminine
Element: Air, Water, Fire
Planet: Venus
Zodiac: Sagittarius

<u>Deities:</u> Venus, Thor, Freya, Cerridwen, Brigid, Lugh, Angus Mac Og, the Dagda

CEDAR
(CEDRUS SPP, THUJA SPP, JUNIPERUS SPP)

<u>Common North American species:</u> Alaska cedar, eastern red cedar, Texas cedar, western red cedar, white cedar

<u>Range of native habitat:</u> Northeastern, Southeastern, Southern, Midwestern, Western, Southwestern U.S., Pacific Northwest, Alaska; Eastern and far Western Canada

The aromatic evergreens known as "cedar" can be confusing to discuss, since most trees called "cedar" in North America are not "true" cedars (genus Cedrus), but are actually other conifers belonging to either the genus Juniperus or the genus Thuja.

In fact, none of the four Cedrus species are native to North America. (However, the Atlas Cedar (*Cedrus Atlantica*) was introduced

60

into the U.S. in the mid-nineteenth century, and has been cultivated as an ornamental tree ever since.) The trees in North America known as "cedar" have traits in common with the true cedars (such as appearance and aromatic wood), and so were misnamed by early pioneers in regions where these trees grow.

All three of these tree types (Cedrus, Juniperus, and Thuja) are related in that they belong to the order Pinales, which includes all conifers. In this guide, "true" cedar is considered synonymous with the others, since we now have a history of understanding these various trees as cedar, and thus have collectively manifested a sameness between them. This bears out in the similarities between magical purposes and associations for all of these trees. However, you can find more magical uses by researching each species of "cedar" on its own.

Like many conifers, cedar represents renewal and eternal life. Cedar is one of the first trees to return to areas that have been burned or cleared of vegetation, and is used medicinally by some Native American women to restore strength after giving birth. The smoke of burning cedar has been used by native North Americans for millennia in sacred ceremonies, and to repel malevolent spirits. Cedar's preservative properties were employed by the ancient Celts on the severed heads of their defeated enemies (the head being seen as the "seat of the soul" in Celtic culture), and by Egyptians in the embalming process.

In aromatherapy, cedar oil helps to lift depression and banish stress, returning one's ability to access a spiritual outlook. Communing physically with cedar trees, whether through using the essential oil, carrying a sprig in your pocket, or sitting against the trunk of a cedar, is an excellent way to rejuvenate your personal energy, particularly after experiencing hardship or expending great effort on an endeavor.

Cedar's magical properties include purification, protection, and positive energy, as well as communing with divine wisdom. It is used in charms for longevity, protection, luck, and prosperity. Cedar wands and smudge sticks are used to cleanse negative energy from homes and sacred spaces. Red cedar is particularly known for assisting with divination and finding clarity in confusing situations, as well as improving communication in general.

Magical workings related to psychic protection, banishing nightmares, connecting with helpful spirits, regaining and retaining good health, and creating sacred space can all benefit from incorporating cedar.

Magical Associations:

Gender: Masculine
Element: Fire, Earth, Air
Planet: Sun, Jupiter, Mars, Mercury
Zodiac: Leo, Gemini, Virgo
Deities: Ra, Artemis, Persephone, Jupiter

ELM
(ULMUS SPP)

Common North American species: American elm, rock elm, slippery elm, winged elm

Range of native habitat: Northeastern, Southeastern, Midwestern, Southern, and parts of Western U.S.; Eastern and parts of Western Canada

The graceful elm can grow to be up to 150 feet tall, and has dark green leaves 4 to 6 inches in length. Its upward-reaching branches often create a canopy that resembles a vase or an inverted triangle.

Unfortunately, elms are highly susceptible to a fungus spread by the elm bark beetle. Known as Dutch Elm disease, this fungus has caused the elm to become an endangered tree. However, elms can still be found throughout their native range in North America, and those in areas unaffected by Dutch elm disease can live for several hundred years.

Many trees are associated with fairies and other nature spirits, but elm has a particular association with the elves (or *álfar* in Old Norse), a mysterious race of invisible beings that dwell in various landscapes throughout Germanic mythology. The Anglo-Saxons referred to the elm as "Elven," and this tree is still considered one to visit if you'd like to make contact with the wood elves. (Legends tell us this can be accomplished by sitting under an elm at night and singing until dawn.)

In both Greek and Celtic myth, the elm appears in relation to the Underworld, and it has indeed been one of the most frequently used trees in making coffins. Elm also has an interesting association with Witches—it is said that in Britain, the species known as "wych elm" was named so because Witches met under this tree.

One species of elm popular in herbal medicine from past to present is slippery elm. The inner bark of this tree can be used to treat colds, coughs, and sore throats. It can be applied externally to cuts and scrapes, and drunk as a tea to help speed the healing of broken bones. Slippery elm tea is also good for nausea and menstrual issues. In tree essence form, English elm helps dispel depression and anxiety, rejuvenates the mind and sharpens the sixth sense.

Elm is used for a variety of magical purposes, including love, protection, stability, connection with nature spirits, and connecting with the divine feminine. To attract love, make a charm using elm wood and/or flowers and wear it around your neck. You can also use ground elm in a love incense blend, or place two small elm branches on your altar for any love-related workings. For protection, powdered slippery elm bark can be sprinkled in the corners of each room, or carried in a sachet in your pocket.

Traditionally, elm protects against malicious gossip, and sticks of it can be tied together with a yellow cord and burned for this purpose. Use elm in workings related to fertility and/or rebirth, and in rituals honoring the Goddess, especially in her Crone aspect. To add stability or focus to any spell, ground yourself after ritual and magic, or gain assistance when navigating any kind of difficult transition, call on the comforting energy of this gentle tree.

Magical Associations:

Gender: Feminine
Element: Air, Water, Earth
Planet: Mercury, Saturn
Zodiac: Capricorn, Pisces
Deities: Orpheus, Dionysus, Hecate, Gaia, Odin, Loki, Cerridwen, Danu, the Crone Goddess

FIR
(ABIES SPP)

Common North American species: balsam fir, Colorado fir, Fraser fir, giant fir, noble fir, red fir, Rocky Mountain fir, white fir

Range of native habitat: Northeastern, parts of Southeastern and Midwestern, Northwestern, Southwestern U.S., Alaska; all regions of Canada

The fir belongs to the genus Abies, and is a part of the larger pine family (pinaceae), but is distinguishable from pine in that its needles are typically short (just 1 to 1.5 inches) and grow in pairs opposite each other on the stem, rather than in bundles. Their cones usually grow in upright cylinders. Some species of fir have prickly needles, while others do not—so be careful when approaching a fir for the first time!

One of many coniferous evergreens associated with immortality and the continuity of life, the fir tree was sacred to ancient deities like

Artemis, a Greek goddess of childbirth, and Osiris, the Egyptian god who was killed by his jealous brother and then resurrected his wife, Isis.

Interestingly, the fir is also a popular choice for celebrating the Christmas holiday—the birth point of yet another birth-death-resurrection cycle. The Christmas tree tradition actually stems from ancient pagan Europe, where evergreen trees were part of mid-winter ceremonies from as far south as Greece to the northern reaches of Norse and Germanic lands.

The fir tree was also highly valued by the Druids and by various Native American tribes, who view it as a protective tree. Some use fir branches for flooring in sacred sweat lodges. Balsam fir trees have also been used in "weather sticks," branches that indicate humidity levels, which can be used to predict rain. It is said that the silver fir has a similar use, but it's the cones which indicate wet or dry weather approaching.

The resin and essential oils from the buds of fir have been used medicinally to treat coughs and other respiratory issues, as well as rheumatism and gout, and to seal wounds. Fir needles can be steeped in a tea to provide extra vitamin C when fighting colds, or in the bath for soothing symptoms of rheumatism. The inner bark of some fir species is also effective for treating chest congestion and fevers. Some fir species are poisonous to animals, and the essential oil can be irritating to the skin, so approach medicinal use of fir with caution.

Fir's magical properties make it excellent for use in workings relating to childbirth, healing, energizing the body, and regeneration. Its needles are burned to mitigate labor pains and in ceremonies to bless mother and baby after childbirth. They can also be burned to lift negative energy from a space in order to lighten one's mood, and the tree essence aids with creativity and feelings of empowerment.

Fir's association with regeneration and with insight makes it a good Dark Moon tree—commune with a fir as you seek clarity on what needs to be released in your life in order to make room for new blessings. It is also used in spellwork for youth and vitality, and bringing about or adjusting to change.

Fir is also used in prosperity magic. Place needles or cones in charms to carry in your pocket or purse for this purpose. If possible, work a prosperity spell in the presence of a fir tree, or bring its branches to your indoor altar. It can be added to charms for protection and increasing personal power, and in spells related to healing karmic issues. Use fir resin instead of wax to seal any spell involving words written on folded pieces of paper, or in place of glue in magical crafts. And of course, fir is a perfect tree for use in Yule/Winter Solstice celebrations!

Magical Associations:

Gender: Feminine
Element: Earth
Planet: Moon, Jupiter, Pluto
Zodiac: Capricorn, Cancer
Deities: Osiris, Artemis, Diana, the Triple Goddess

HAWTHORN
(CRATAEGUS SPP)

<u>Common North American species:</u> black hawthorn, blueberry hawthorn, cockspur hawthorn, green hawthorn, mayhaw, parsley hawthorn, riverflat hawthorn, Washington hawthorn, willow hawthorn

<u>Range of native habitat:</u> all regions of the continental U.S. (including Alaska); Eastern, Western, and parts of Northern Canada

Hawthorn is a smaller tree, often appearing as a bush but capable of growing to heights of between 30 and 40 feet. It produces white flowers in spring and bright red-purple berries in autumn, and has sharp thorns growing from its branches or trunk. In prior centuries, the thorns made it a favorite for growing in hedgerows to keep out thieves. Hawthorn leaves are generally oval shaped but in some species more closely resemble oak leaves.

Hawthorn was associated with marriage across cultures in ancient Europe. In parts of Greece, newly married couples wore crowns with the blossoms, while the other celebrants carried torches made from the branches. In the British Isles, the couples would dance around a hawthorn tree to bless their union.

The tree had another highly important function, as the official signal of the start of summer, and thus the time for Beltane celebrations. (Hawthorn blossoms in May, and in the years prior to the adoption of the Gregorian calendar this typically occurred at the start of the month.) The blossoms were woven into crowns and garlands worn by the Beltane revelers. Hawthorn is also known as "the May Tree," and was incorporated into May Day celebrations as the tree used for the maypole.

Hawthorn was also the subject of many taboos and other folk beliefs. Along with oak and ash, hawthorn is one of the fairy triad, meaning that wherever these three trees grow together, the fairies are likely to dwell. A lone hawthorn is perhaps even more enchanted, as it was believed to mark the boundary between the material and fairy worlds, especially if found near a well or spring. Harming such a tree in any way could bring severe misfortune.

Furthermore, while hawthorn branches could be used to decorate the yard for the summer festivities, it was taboo to bring it into the house, which was said to risk illness and death. Hawthorn also symbolized death for some Germanic tribes, who used the wood in funeral pyres.

Hawthorn's medicinal properties are found in the flowers, leaves, berries, and bark, and are useful for heart and blood pressure issues, circulatory disorders, migraines, sore throats, and menopausal symptoms. The flowers and bark are also used as sedatives. The berries contain vitamins B and C, and can be made (along with the blossoms) into wine and jelly. Hawthorn leaves are also edible.

Magically, hawthorn is used in workings related to fertility, purity, marriage, protection, patience, confidence, and creativity. The tree essence promotes forgiveness and love, releasing negativity from the heart center, making hawthorn an excellent tree for healing issues in a marriage. Use the blossoms in early summer in spellwork related to finding a serious romantic partner. Use the berries in fertility magic.

Hawthorn's protective properties work particularly well against negative psychic vibrations, and, like holly, it is also thought to protect against lightning. Placing hawthorn outside near doors and windows guards against unwanted influences, as does growing it in a hedge. Hawthorn is also a purifier, used in smudge sticks to energetically clear new houses, sacred space, and rooms where a person has been ill.

Wands of hawthorn are excellent for magic related to creativity and self-confidence, and gaining insight into a complex situation. Workings related to weather, happiness, good luck, and breaking unwanted habits also benefit from hawthorn's energies. Add the flowers, berries, or bark shavings to sachets and other charms for these purposes. Try using the thorns to carve symbols into candles in lieu of a crystal point or pin, particularly in a spell relating to any of hawthorn's magical associations.

Magical Associations:

Gender: Feminine
Element: Water, Air, Earth
Planet: Mars
Zodiac: Taurus, Cancer
Deities: Hera, Flora, Venus, Olwen, Brigid

HOLLY
(ILEX SPP)

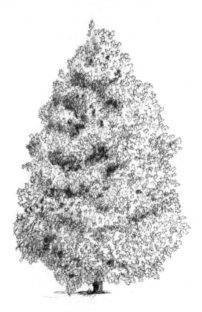

<u>Common North American species:</u> American holly, Carolina holly, myrtle-leaved holly, mountain holly (shrub), winterberry (shrub)

<u>Range of native habitat:</u> Northeastern, Southeastern, Southern, Midwestern U.S.; parts of Eastern Canada

Ilex, or holly, is a large and very widespread genus, with over 400 species of trees and shrubs found in many different places around the world. American holly grows naturally in shaded woods and on the banks of streams and rivers, but various species of holly are also cultivated as hedges around homes and estates.

A cheerful plant whether in shrub, hedge, or tree form, holly is a symbol of luck, good fortune, and eternal life. Holly has always been particularly appreciated in northern climates, where its bright green leaves and red berries provide some much-needed color in the otherwise white and grey landscapes of wintertime.

In some places, predictions about the coming winter were made based on the numbers of holly berries emerging on the trees. If there were more berries than usual, a colder, harder winter was expected.

Holly was also viewed as a protective tree and therefore a tree not to be cut down or burned. (However, harvesting boughs for decoration was allowed.) In particular, holly protected against bad luck, evil spirits, and lightning, and was therefore a desirable tree to plant near one's home. It is now believed that the holly leaves themselves, with their prickly spines, may act as conductors of lightning, drawing the electricity away from nearby objects.

The Druids revered holly and used it for decoration at the Winter Solstice and during the winter months. It was said that bringing holly into the home was an invitation to the faeries to come in and shelter from the cold. The energy of the holly kept the faeries and the humans comfortably out of each other's way in the cozy, small space.

In Scotland, people placed holly branches outside the house to keep evil at bay. Holly was also important to the Norse. It was associated with Thor, the god of thunder and lightning, and in some myths it is said that Odin's sacred spear was made of holly. The ancient Romans celebrated Saturnalia with boughs of holly, giving them as gifts to their friends.

One species of holly from the Brazilian rainforest provides the leaves for yerba mate, a naturally caffeinated tea that many find to be uplifting to the spirit. However, many species of holly are poisonous to humans and the berries in particular are dangerous to children. This may be why holly's medicinal properties are rarely employed by modern herbalists, but we do know that the leaves and bark were used among Native Americans as an emetic (to induce vomiting) and to heal psychological and emotional imbalances.

The flower and tree essences of holly help to dispel negative emotions like jealousy and the desire for revenge, and give support to the process of opening the heart and restoring peace of mind. Holly can be used in magic related to balancing emotions and finding balance in the midst of busy days, reenergizing during the dark days of winter, and victory over challenging situations.

It is also effective in workings for love, attraction, and fertility, and can be carried in a sachet by men who wish to attract women. The leaves and berries make useful allies in any spellwork, whether as active ingredients or as energetic "assistants" on the altar.

If you're looking to plant a hedge around the perimeter of your property, holly creates a strong yet attractive protective shield. Planting a holly tree creates a fairy-friendly yard and a place to spend time communing with the Otherworld. Bring boughs of holly into the house for Yule celebrations, and then burn the dried greens at Imbolc to welcome in the new growing season.

<u>Magical Associations:</u>

<u>Gender:</u> Masculine, Feminine
<u>Element:</u> Fire
<u>Planet:</u> Mars, Saturn
<u>Zodiac:</u> Leo, Sagittarius
<u>Deities:</u> Lugh, Thor, Mars, Govannon, Goibniu

MAPLE
(ACER SPP)

Common North American species: boxelder, red maple, silver maple, sugar maple

Range of native habitat: all regions of the continental U.S (including Alaska); Eastern, Western, and much of Northern Canada

Maples have distinctively-shaped leaves, and are one of the few native North American deciduous trees with an opposite branching arrangement, meaning that the leaves and buds grow directly across from each other on each side of the stem, rather than alternating up the sides. There are over 100 species of maple, with varying height ranges, but the average mature maple in North America reaches between 50 and 100 feet.

Maples are native to both Europe and North America (as well as Asia), but the European pagan traditions seem not to have viewed maple as a go-to magical tree. However, for those in the U.S. and

Canada who have witnessed maple's annual display of stunningly vivid leaf coloring, or tasted the sweetness of pure maple syrup, it's clear that Nature imbued this lovely tree with plenty of magic.

In fact, the five-pointed leaves of some species of maple are even reminiscent of the star inside the pentacle, a symbol much-revered by Wiccans and other Witches. And the annual cycle of the sugar maple, whose sap runs in the spring and whose leaves flame gloriously before leaving the branches bare for winter, makes for an excellent living symbol of the Wheel of the Year.

On a symbolic level, maple has been said to stand for generosity, abundance, success, balance, and practicality. Medicinally, the inner bark has been used to treat coughs and digestive issues, while treatments for sore eyes have been created from the bark and the sap. Maple leaves can be packed around apples and root vegetables to help preserve them into the colder months. Maple tree essence assists with finding balance, self-sufficiency, and unconditional love of life.

The syrup of the sugar, red, or black maple is perhaps the most well-known and widely accessible magical ingredient that maple provides. Used in kitchen witchery for love and money magic, maple syrup also has the advantage of being a healthier and more nutritious alternative to sugar. This underscores one of maple's subtle spiritual messages—that it's beneficial for us to allow sweetness and joy into our lives.

Use maple syrup in magic for attracting love, mending a strained relationship, or soothing a troubled mind. Or, charm an entire bottle of it for a "prosperity syrup" that you can use daily on pancakes, in smoothies, etc. Just be sure to check the label before you buy, as much of what is sold as "maple syrup" in grocery stores is just flavored corn syrup. (Hint: if it's cheap, it's not real maple syrup.)

Maple has been called the "traveler's wood," perhaps because it was used by many indigenous North American tribes to make paddles and oars. Add a small twig or strip of maple bark to a travel charm for extra luck and comfort. A wand of maple is ideal for those who are constantly on the move, as well as those who appreciate beauty, harmony, and storytelling.

Many musical instruments are made from maple wood, going back at least as far as the Anglo-Saxon period in Britain, which illustrates maple's association with beauty and harmony. Use the leaves, twigs, or bark in any spellwork centered on drawing these qualities into your life. Maple is also useful in magical workings related to intellectual pursuits, communication, and decisions, especially those involving a change in your situation.

Magical Associations:

Gender: Feminine, Masculine
Element: Spirit, Water, Earth
Planet: Moon, Jupiter, Neptune
Zodiac: Libra, Virgo
Deities: Danu, Hera, any lunar goddess

OAK
(QUERCUS SPP)

Common North American species: bur oak, live oak, red oak, water oak, white oak

Range of native habitat: Northeastern, Southeastern, Southern, Midwestern, Western U.S., Pacific Northwest; Eastern and most of Western Canada

The oak is one of the most majestic trees in the Northern Hemisphere. Its graceful, wide-reaching branches create an impressive canopy of distinctly-shaped leaves, and it can reach heights of between 80 and 100 feet. Often the canopy is nearly as wide as the height of the tree.

Oak's size and longevity (some species live an average of 300 years), along with the many benefits it provides to humans and animals alike, have led it to be considered "the king of the forest" in many cultures. It is also a beloved symbol of the Hermetic principle of "as above, so below," since its underground root system tends to mirror the spread of its branches.

In Rome, the "mighty oak" was symbolic of military strength, and victorious military leaders wore crowns of oak leaves when celebrating their wins. Oak was associated with powerful leader gods across several cultures, including Greek, Roman, Celtic, and ancient Germanic deities. It was also associated with gods of thunder and lightning, perhaps due to its propensity to be struck by lightning, and often enough, survive to grow even taller and wider.

The Druids, who as we saw in Part One held their rituals in oak groves, believed that the mistletoe found in some oak trees was left there by divine lightning strikes. The Druids were also known to eat acorns as part of their divination practices.

Oak was important to our pagan ancestors in both magical and more mundane realms. The acorns fed early settlers in Britain, as well as their livestock, and oak wood was highly useful for building housing and furniture as well as a consistent source of firewood.

Folk traditions of the British Isles held that oak had magical healing abilities, and some believed that walking around the trunk of a living oak would cure what ailed them, as the first bird to alight on the tree afterward would carry off their sickness. A widely known folk custom holds that catching a falling oak leaf in autumn will protect you from colds and flu all winter long.

Oak bark has been used medicinally as an astringent to treat bowel issues and fever, as well as sore throat, inflamed gums, eczema, and aches and bruises. One treatment for frostbite called for boiling oak leaves that had wintered over while still attached to the tree. Acorns are rich in B vitamins, calcium, and potassium and can be taken medicinally to improve metabolism, support bone health, and prevent diabetes.

Magically, oak is symbolic of strength, prosperity, and fertility. Its longevity and ability to survive hardships such as lightning, drought, and fire also evoke the qualities of courage, wisdom, and endurance. It is excellent for workings related to wisdom in authority, personal sovereignty, protection, longevity, abundance, and fertility, as well as finding the truth underneath confusing situations.

Oak's magic can be harnessed from its bark, timber, leaves, and/or acorns. Use the bark in incense and sachets, or carry it in your wallet or purse for protection, abundance, and fertility. Burn the leaves for purification, or use them in healing and protection spells, or any working involving victory. Wear a leaf around your neck (under your shirt) to be able to perceive when others are being untruthful. Add a few leaves to your bath for healing emotional issues and gaining strength and fortitude to deal with challenges.

Acorns are instant magical charms in and of themselves. Charge them and keep them in your pocket, or add them to sachets and Witch jars for any purpose, but especially for prosperity, wealth, fertility, and protection from illness. It is said that acorns are best gathered at night for fertility work, and planted during the Dark Moon for prosperity. Place them in windowsills to protect the home and attract good fortune.

Oak is one of the most energetically radiant trees, and ideal for meditating under and attuning to the spirits within it. Connect with an oak to help find focus in the midst of distractions, or when you're seeking comfort from the benevolent energies of Mother Nature.

PINE
(PINUS SPP)

Common North American species: Eastern white pine, loblolly pine, lodgepole pine, longleaf pine, pinyon pine, pitch pine, ponderosa pine, Western white pine

Range of native habitat: all regions of continental U.S. (including Alaska) and Canada

The genus Pinus is a plentiful one, with over 90 species of trees covering a wide range of habitats. Pines grow in the Arctic as well as in the desert and the tropics, so it's safe to assume that anyone anywhere wishing to connect magically with a pine will have little trouble finding one. Typically, pines are tall, coniferous evergreens, with heights averaging between 50 and 80 feet. They are recognizable from other conifers by their bundles of long, needle-like leaves and generally larger cones.

Sacred to the Druids and many native North American peoples, the pine tree has plenty of history, lore, and magical traditions on both sides of the Atlantic. Pine is listed among the seven "Nobles of the Wood" in medieval Irish records, and is considered a symbol of peace among the Iroquois tribes.

Some species of pine are extremely long lived, as we can see from the bristlecone pines in California, which are nearly 5,000 years old. Pines are also quite hardy—they even survived the last Ice Age in some places, and were among the first plants to flourish afterward. Perhaps the Druids, who burned pine at the winter solstice and decorated live pine trees with shiny objects, were aware of the strength and resilience of this mighty evergreen.

Pine needles have been used medicinally to relieve congestion and heal kidney and bladder issues. A bath made with the needles and cones can help with breathing and skin problems. Essential oil of pine is also helpful for clearing the sinuses, as well as relieving sore muscles and joints, and has antiviral and antiseptic properties. (Note: be cautious with this oil as it can irritate the skin and mucus membranes.)

Pine oil has an uplifting and energizing effect in aromatherapeutic applications, and is useful in cleaning products. Nutritionally, pine is prized for its needles, which contain more vitamin C than lemons, and its seeds (known as "pine nuts"), which contain vitamin E, magnesium, and potassium. The nuts are also delicious in pesto!

Symbolically, pine represents immortality, rebirth, health, fertility, strength (especially during hard times), and prosperity. It is used magically for purification, protection, fertility, renewal, longevity, and good fortune.

Use a wand of pine in ritual and spellwork for any of these purposes, or in magic that uses only gestures and no spoken words. Attach a pine cone to the tip of any wand to enhance divine masculine energy and fertility. Carry pine cones to increase healthy longevity as well as fertility (pine nuts, needles, and bark also work for fertility). For protection, burn pine needles in the fire. Place a pine branch over your bed to keep illness away. To banish negativity from any space, burn pine incense or essential oil, or use pine oil in a cleaning solution for floors, walls, or laundry.

You can also use a pine branch as a besom to sweep out negative energy from indoor or outdoor spaces. A purification bath with pine needles raises energy and fosters clarity over troubling issues, as does meditating at the base of a pine tree. Use pine nuts in kitchen witchery for increased prosperity, and hang a pine branch over your front door to maintain good fortune.

Magical Associations:

Gender: Masculine, Feminine
Element: Air, Fire, Earth, Spirit
Planet: Mars, Jupiter, Saturn
Zodiac: Cancer, Capricorn
Deities: Isis, Artemis, Pan, Ariadne, Rhea, Diana, Dionysus

ROWAN (MOUNTAIN ASH)
(SORBUS SPP)

<u>Common North American species:</u> American mountain ash, Cascade mountain ash, Greene's mountain ash, northern mountain ash

<u>Range of native habitat:</u> Northeastern, Southeastern, Midwestern, Northwestern, and Southwestern U.S., Alaska; Eastern, Western, and parts of Northern Canada

Rowan is often referred to as "mountain ash," particularly in North America, due to its smooth bark, upward-reaching branches, and compound leaves, which are similar to that of ash. However, the two are not botanically related, and rowan is typically a much shorter tree, reaching average heights of 10 to 30 feet.

The "mountain" descriptor comes from rowan's ability to grow at high elevations and endure harsh conditions, often sprouting up from cracks between rocks where birds have dropped seeds from the berries. The elevations at which they can grow and the bright red hues of its berries may have been what led some ancient Celts to believe that rowan provided food for the *aos sidhe*, or the fairy race.

Rowan's status as a magical tree may also be due in part to the unique five-pointed star appearing on each of its red berries, a symbol of protection in many ancient traditions. For the Celts, rowan was particularly associated with protection from negative magic, of both human and fairy origins. Rowans were planted near the front door of homes to protect the house and all who dwelled within. Rowan wood was used to kindle fires to protect cattle from fairies. Sprigs were hung at Beltane above doorways, children's cradles, and butter churns (to keep the fairies from spoiling the butter). Protective charms were made from its twigs.

Druids utilized the rowan for magical craft, ritual, and divination, using the bark and berries to dye ritual garments and the wood for funereal fires. Ceremonial cakes were cooked over fires of rowan wood. Twigs were used for divining for metals, and were crushed into incense for use in divination. Rowan was considered so sacred in Scotland that its wood was traditionally never used for anything but ritual purposes. The Scandinavians also saw rowan as protective, and planted trees near their farm buildings to secure protection for crops and animals against storms and other damage. Rowans that grew in the most unlikely or inaccessible places were considered to be the most powerful, and were referred to as "flying rowan."

The tree was sacred to Thor because it once saved him from drowning in a river by bending over so he could grab hold of it. In some translations of Norse mythology it is the rowan, rather than the elm, that the first woman was made from. Some contemporary Norse pagan traditions hold that the ancient rune masters used rowan branches to carve runes for divination. Interestingly, the English word "rowan" shares its origin with the Old Norse word *runa*, which translates to "a secret" or "to whisper."

Rowan berries contain large amounts of vitamin C, and were used to prevent and treat scurvy. Ripe berries have diuretic and purgative properties, and the bark was used to soothe upset stomachs. The berries have also been made into wine, ale, and spirits, as well as jelly.

They do contain an acid that is toxic when the berries are raw, but becomes safe once they are cooked.

Magically, rowan is still used today in workings related to protection, as well as psychic ability and insight, healing, and positivity. It is still planted in yards to protect the home from negative vibrations, and to bring the blessing of the fairies. To make a traditional protection charm, place two rowan twigs in an equal-armed cross and secure it with red thread. Keep one in your home and/or bring one with you when traveling.

Rowan berries are specifically useful in amulets and charm bags for strength, power and healing. The tree's hardiness in nature makes it a symbol of beauty, grace, and perseverance in the face of challenges. Rowan is also excellent for workings related to psychic perception and attunement to nature.

Add the bark to incense to burn during divination, and hold a wand or staff (or walking stick) of rowan while hiking through the forest to connect more deeply with the spirits and energies of the forest. Meditate under a rowan tree to strengthen your ability to hear your inner wisdom. If you don't have access to rowan trees, the tree essence can have similar effects.

WILLOW
(SALIX SPP)

Common North American species: black willow, gray willow, feltleaf willow, Pacific willow, peachleaf willow

Range of native habitat: all regions of continental U.S. (including Alaska); all regions of Canada

The genus Salix contains over 400 species of trees and shrubs and is extremely widespread in North America, meaning that wherever you live, you should be able to locate at least one kind of willow, whether it be a stately tree or something on the smaller side. Willows typically have narrow, elongated leaves, slender branches, and soft, pliant wood.

The most well-known species is probably the weeping willow, which is found as an ornamental tree in many parks, gardens, and yards, but this tree is actually native to Asia. North American willows can be just as graceful in appearance, but their branches do not "droop" downward like those of weeping willows.

The word "willow" shares linguistic roots with the word "witch" in the ancient Indo-European language, and indeed the tree itself has been associated with both Moon and Crone goddesses among the ancient Greeks, Romans, and Celts alike.

The Greek mythical poet Orpheus was said to have received his creative gifts after touching the willows in a sacred grove, and he carried willow branches with him as he traveled through the Underworld. Willows growing near wells were sometimes turned into "wishing trees" in Celtic areas, particularly when the wish was for healing from the grief of a broken heart.

The willow's connections with wisdom, mystery, death, and the afterlife seem to go back to prehistoric times. This may be at least in part because willows are often found near water, which in turn links this tree with the Moon. The afterlife association may also be due to willow's regenerative abilities—a cut branch planted in the ground can quickly grow into a new tree.

In Celtic myth, the willow also plays an important role in creation itself—it was in a willow tree that two scarlet snake eggs were hidden, one containing the Sun and the other containing the Earth, until the eggs hatched and the full cosmos came into being.

In the medicinal realm, willow is best known for a component in its bark known as salicin, which is the primary ingredient in aspirin. Prior to the invention of aspirin, young willow twigs were chewed for pain relief. The bark has also been used to treat rheumatism, colds, and fever. Willow sap can be used to reduce acne, and the leaves and bark can be boiled and used as a treatment for dandruff.

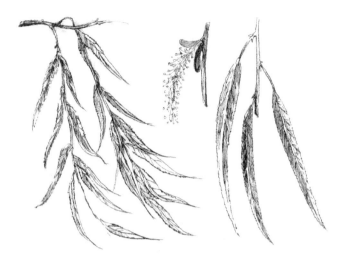

In the magical realm, willow is symbolic of renewal and immortality, again due to its ability to regenerate from a broken branch. It is also associated with resolving or healing grief, as its "otherworldly" yet reassuring energy reminds us that we are all eternal beings. Due to its quick rate of growth, willow also assists with magic concerning vitality, and its association with the Moon makes it excellent for workings related to cyclical change. In fact, willow is good for all Moon-related magic in any phase of the lunar cycle.

Use willow in spells, rituals, or other workings related to letting go of relationships and/or old hurts, accepting loss, and making way for renewal in the form of new blessings coming into your life. Willow can also be used in spells for love and healing. Crush the leaves and bark to use in incense for these purposes, or charm a piece of bark to carry with you until your goal has manifested.

Willow makes good dowsing wands for finding water. Furthermore, it is said that willow's wood naturally aligns with the energy raised in magical work, making it an excellent choice for wands in general, and especially for those just starting out in the Craft. Willow's watery, lunar properties also make it ideal for workings related to psychic ability, divination, and astral travel. Try placing three willow leaves under your pillow for clear, informative dreams. Sit under a willow tree and meditate, and/or write in your journal about an issue that's been troubling you—especially matters of the heart—and ask the spirit of the tree for guidance.

Magical Associations:

<u>Gender:</u> Feminine
<u>Element:</u> Water
<u>Planet:</u> Moon
<u>Zodiac:</u> Cancer, Scorpio
<u>Deities:</u> Persephone, Hera, Hecate, Ceres, Artemis, Selene, Luna, Diana, Minerva, Cerridwen, Brighid, Arianrhod, Rhiannon, the Morrigan

YEW
(TAXUS SPP)

<u>Common North American species:</u> Pacific yew (also Florida yew, endangered)

Range of native habitat: Florida (very small area), Western U.S, Pacific Northwest, Alaska; Western Canada

There are only eight species of yew trees, and most are not native to North America. However, because there is one species still found in the western U.S. and Canada, and because yew is highly significant in the lore of our ancestors in the Craft, it is included in this guide. European yew has been widely adopted as an ornamental tree in the U.S., so you don't necessarily have to live in the West to find a yew in your area.

Among magical trees, yew has perhaps one of the most mysterious energies. This may be due in part to its capacity to live for thousands of years, but also its unusual ability to "rebirth" itself. Indeed, its own branches can grow down under the ground and form new trunks, which then emerge from within the hollowed-out central trunk of the original tree.

This phenomenon makes it difficult to tell a given yew's age, since the tree rings of the original trunk are destroyed by the new growth. However, one particularly ancient yew found in Scotland has been estimated to be at least five thousand years old. At any rate, it should come as no surprise that the yew has been associated since ancient times with longevity, rebirth, regeneration, and reincarnation—by the Greeks, Celts, and Germanic peoples alike.

The ancient Irish Celts understood the mighty longevity of the yew, and it was considered to be one of the oldest living beings on the Earth. Irish mythology tells us that yew was brought to the Emerald Isle from the Otherworld, one of five sacred trees that helped establish the ancient kingdoms of Ireland.

It was also named as one of the Seven Chieftain Trees of Brehon law in pre-Christian times, so anyone trimming a yew risked bad luck and even punishment. Yew was seen as a symbol of death and resurrection, and the leaves were placed on graves to affirm that a new life awaited the recently departed.

The Germanic peoples also revered the yew, associating it with the Winter Solstice as well as with death and rebirth. The ancient runes Eihwaz and Yr represented both the tree and its regenerative powers. In fact, several old European names for yew can be traced back etymologically to words meaning "eternal," showing that the timeless quality of the yew has always been recognized.

Yews are also well known in Europe for their presence in ancient churchyards, particularly in the British Isles, many of which are presumed to predate Christianity. While some of these trees may indeed have been planted during Christian times, many are likely traceable to pagan days, when yews marked sacred spaces, or portals to the underworld.

Yews are extremely toxic and therefore not used medicinally, with one exception—extracts of yew have been discovered to treat certain forms of cancer. Aside from this, yew is not physically beneficial to humans. Magically, however, yew is a powerful ally, and can assist with workings related to knowledge, wisdom, spiritual growth, protection, transformation, psychic abilities, strength, and rebirth.

A branch of yew makes for an excellent wand or even dowsing rod, and can be held in your hands to enhance spirit communication and astral travel. Many who work with runes or the Ogham for divination purposes love to carve these symbols into small yew twigs, as yew has been associated with divination and shamanic mysteries in both Druid and Norse traditions. (Just be sure to keep such items away from children or pets who may be tempted to chew on them!)

Yew's reputation for being a tree "between worlds" may be connected, at least in part, to the hallucinogenic gas the bark can emit on warm days. If you have access to a yew tree, you might try meditating near it on a warm sunny afternoon. (Depending on your sensitivity, you might want to have someone to check in with you at an agreed-upon time, just to make sure you don't overdo it.)

If you don't live near any yew trees, you can still call upon its mystical properties through visualization and/or focusing on an image of a yew. For help in releasing a difficult situation, imagine re-rooting your life path with the branches of your current circumstances. What "failures" or "deaths" have you experienced that could be regenerated into something new and positive?

Magical Associations:

Gender: Feminine
Element: Earth, Water
Planet: Saturn, Pluto, Jupiter
Zodiac: Scorpio
Deities: Artemis, Persephone, Hecate, Odin, Banbha, the Morrigan, the Crone Goddess

THE WISDOM
OF THE FOREST

Trees make for excellent illustrations of the interconnectedness of Nature, the forces of light and shadow, and the power of the unseen. The tallest trees in a forest absorb the most sunlight, while their canopies of leaves and branches block much of the light from the forest floor. This means smaller trees and bushes are left unable to reach the same heights as the great old giants.

Yet trees, shrubs, and plants of all heights and sizes play their part in the overall ecosystem. Many of these forest inhabitants need the shade of their taller neighbors in order to survive and thrive. And each species serves different kinds of birds, insects, and other forest animals in terms of food and shelter. In the diverse and interweaving variety of life in the forest, we can see how Nature co-creates with itself, for the benefit of all.

Yet, like the forces at play in any magical working, this interconnectedness goes beyond what we can see on the surface. Birds hide their nests in the safety of leafy branches, and hollowed out logs and trunks from fallen trees shelter all kinds of animals. Furthermore, behind their exterior layer of bark, trees are teeming with activity as they move nutrients and water throughout their bodily system.

Trees even send messages to each other in the form of chemical compounds and electrical impulses, through an underground network of fungi that connects the trees from their roots. Through this network they can warn each other about insects on the attack, and will actually share nutrients with any struggling neighbor trees.

The forest offers a useful metaphor for considering the interconnected forces at work in our own lives. When seeking to form an appropriate magical goal, we can consider the possibilities of light and shadow, the perceivable and the unseen, and the hidden connections within the situation at hand.

For example, if you're wishing for a romantic partner but seem to be having no luck, you might meditate on what aspects of yourself you are allowing to grow and expand. Are you reaching for the sun and allowing yourself to bask in the light? Or are you sheltering somewhat comfortably in the shadow of old beliefs about not being "good enough" for a loving relationship?

Perhaps there are old, stale energies left over from past partners that need to be uprooted and cleared. Maybe there are unhealed emotional or spiritual wounds so entrenched within the soil of your heart that you've forgotten they're there. What underlying issues might you not be seeing that are interconnected with your desire for a relationship?

Whatever your intuition leads you to observe, you can now start to formulate a useful magical intention. It could be for healing past hurts so that you're ready to move on, or the courage and confidence to put yourself out on the dating scene. Or you may gain insight on the qualities you're looking for in a partner, so that you can include them in the wording of your intention, rather than simply requesting "a lover."

Whatever form and intention your magic takes, remember that the Universe is ready to work with you. And never forget that just because you don't see results yet, it doesn't mean nothing is happening beneath the surface!

BRANCHING OUT

Now that you've been introduced to some of the most common magical trees in North America, you can begin connecting with them both physically and metaphysically—through meditation, visualization, and spellwork.

In Part Three, you'll find a diverse collection of ideas and magical workings to inspire and develop your practice, from connecting with trees on the astral plane, to making your own wand, to spells for love, abundance, and protection. So check out this tree-oriented grimoire and, as always, go where your intuition leads you!

PART THREE

AN ARBOREAL GRIMOIRE

ALL-NATURAL MAGIC

Working with the magical gifts of the natural world is a beautifully rewarding way to practice the Craft. Whether you're communing with Nature in a forest, a grove, a park, your back yard, or at your indoor altar, there is great power in tapping into the energies of trees.

The spells, rituals and other workings offered here consist almost exclusively of tree-based ingredients. Many call for hand-gathering the leaves, bark, and other gifts of the trees. However, if you want to work with a tree that doesn't grow in your area, you can find many barks, branches, needles, cones, etc. through online magical shops and herbal medicine suppliers. You can also look up the magical properties of trees near you that aren't included in this guide for appropriate substitutions.

YOU AND THE TREE: AN ENERGETIC PARTNERSHIP

When we set out to incorporate a new magical tool into our practice, such as a new wand or crystal, we always take the time to form an energetic connection with the object first. This typically takes the form of clearing the object of old or unwanted energy and charging it with our own personal energy.

Trees present us with an interesting opportunity to reimagine this practice. As living, growing beings in their own right, trees have their own unique energies that we can choose to attune to in order to co-create with them. Getting in the habit of approaching trees more as "partners" than as "tools" in magic is an important step.

The following two exercises will help you learn to tune into the natural magical energies of trees, both on the physical plane and in the astral realm.

TREE TRUNK EARTHING RITUAL

"Earthing," more traditionally known as "grounding," is a practice used by Witches and modern alternative healers to reconnect the self with the physical body by connecting with the Earth.

Grounding has positive effects on mental, physical, and spiritual health. There are many ways to accomplish grounding, from the simple act of standing with your bare feet in the soil (or sand, if you're on a beach), to laying on the ground, to various visualization processes that bring you into an awareness of your physical body, your connection to Earth, and the present moment.

Grounding is used in Wiccan practice, both before and after ritual, to assist with focus during ritual and transitioning back into "ordinary" reality afterward. The ceremony of cakes and ale is sometimes used as a grounding mechanism, as food helps settle practitioners back into their body after working with intense energies.

Trees provide a powerful resource for grounding, as they emanate a calming, healing presence and are perfect embodiments of being "rooted" in the Earth. This is also a great way to get acquainted with the energies of different species of trees, so you may want to work with a few and note your experiences in a journal to compare. For this ritual, it's ideal to be barefoot, but don't let that stop you from trying it in cold weather—you can keep your shoes on if need be.

Instructions:

Choose a tree with a reasonably large trunk that you can stand right next to. Stand in front of the tree trunk with both feet firmly planted on the ground.

Place your receptive palm (your non-dominant hand) against the tree trunk and hold it there for a few moments, breathing deeply. Notice the subtle changes in the energy of your body. Do you feel calmer? More enlivened? What shifts are taking place?

Now, place your projective palm (your dominant hand) against the trunk, at least a couple of feet away from your other hand. Close your eyes. Visualize the energy of the tree entering through your receptive hand, traveling up through your arm and into your heart center. See it circulating throughout your heart center and slowly spreading throughout the rest of your body. Now see it traveling down through your other arm and exiting through your dominant hand back into the trunk of the tree.

Stay here for a few more moments, breathing deeply, feeling the tree's energy humming throughout your body. When you're ready to release the energy, press both palms firmly into the trunk and silently thank the tree. (You can also give it a hug, if you feel comfortable!) Then take your hands away and shake your arms out gently to release any excess energy.

ENCHANTED FOREST MEDITATION

This visualization exercise is a great way to unwind from a busy day, prepare yourself for magical work (especially tree magic!), and/or cultivate a habit of connecting with the energy of trees when you don't have physical access to any.

Here, you'll be going for an astral hike in the forest. If you don't have much personal experience with forests, you might want to spend some time looking at photographs and/or watching nature documentaries to get better acquainted with the kinds of imagery you can call up during the visualization.

Exercises like these are good practice in co-creating with the Universe in the realm of imagination. For while you'll be creating your own individual forest in your mind's eye, you'll be allowing the details to come through to you from the astral plane.

Note: Conducting a detailed meditation from written text can be a challenge, since you're unlikely to memorize every detail of the instructions before closing your eyes. Instead, try listening to this passage being read aloud, either by a friend or from a voice recording. (Most smart phones have built-in voice recorder apps, plus an audiobook version of this book is available.) If you can't find a friend or a voice recorder, then try copying down the instructions by hand, which will help you to remember them in better detail.

You might try enhancing the experience by playing actual forest sounds in the background (plenty of videos can be found online). And if you're not sure how much time to spend in the visualization, consider setting a timer for 5, 10, or 15 minutes.

The Visualization:

Close your eyes and take a deep breath in. As you exhale, see the beginning of a path into the woods, marked by a sign that reads "Enchanted Forest."

As you step onto the path, take another deep breath in. Slowly release the breath, allowing your mind to quiet a little.

101

Now simply notice the scene in front of you. What trees are here? Look to the tops of the trees—how high up do the tallest ones reach? What can you see of the sky above?

Now scan down slowly from the tops of the trees to the forest floor. What are the first visual details that call your attention? Allow the spirits of the forest to communicate with you through sight and sound, without trying to analyze the messages with the logical part of your brain.

What colors are dominant among the forest here? Notice the individual shades of brown and grey among the trunks of the trees. Are their barks ridged or smooth? What are the shapes of the leaves? What do you see on the ground? What's growing there? Are there fallen trees among the shrubs and other plants? Are there dead leaves slowly decaying and mulching into the soil?

Take another deep inhale through your nose and release it. What does the air smell like? What are the dominant scents your mind is experiencing right now?

What sounds are present? Listen to the sound of your own breath, and then let your audial awareness radiate out further. Listen for the breeze whispering through the leaves. Listen for the calls of birds from nearby, and from deeper into the forest. Do you hear any small animals rustling along the forest floor?

Spend several moments here, simply attuning to the world you are co-creating. When you feel your analytical mind fading into the background and your perceptive mind emerging into your present awareness, begin walking along the path.

As you step deeper into the forest, listen for the sounds of birds. Their calls and chirps are announcing your presence. Listen for rustling of leaves along the forest floor—these are small animals taking refuge from the vibrations of your footsteps. You are being noticed, and even watched, by the inhabitants of the forest. You are now, however temporarily, part of this magical ecosystem. Stay here as long as you like, or until the timer brings your awareness back to the room.

When you're finished with the visualization, consider trying out some new spellwork, writing in your journal, or engaging in some other creative activity. Feel free to return to your unique "astral forest" any time you wish.

You can also use this practice to develop astral connections with specific species of trees that you don't have physical access to. For example, find several photographs of Pacific yews, and then spend time visualizing one of your own co-creation. You can then draw on the tree's subtle energies in your spellwork.

HARVESTING FROM TREES FOR MAGICAL WORK

Whether you're looking to make a wand, or to use bark, leaves, flowers, etc. from a tree for spellwork, it is extremely important to go about the harvesting process carefully and respectfully.

Cutting branches and/or bark from a tree creates an open wound that exposes the tree to bacteria, pests, mold, etc. and can compromise its ability to transport nutrients and water through the networks of its inner bark. Likewise, over-harvesting spring blossoms or summer leaves can inhibit growth and interfere with natural processes like pollination and food production.

For these and other reasons, many Witches prefer to leave a living tree alone, and forage for blossoms, leaves, branches, and strips of bark that the tree has naturally shed. However, this doesn't mean that can't ever harvest magical ingredients from a living tree—it just means that you need to be careful.

Following the guidelines below, and doing further research into the specific tree(s) you want to harvest from, will help ensure that you don't overly disrupt the natural forces that you're seeking to work in harmony with.

Don't:

- Don't cut bark from the trunk of a tree. This can severely compromise the tree's health. In fact, cutting just one strip of bark from the entire circumference of the trunk will likely kill the tree. Instead, remove a small branch (or twig) that you can reach easily, and then harvest the bark from the cut branch.

- Don't pull leaves off the tree by their stems, as this often also pulls off the bud that might otherwise grow into a new branch. Instead, cut a little way down from the end of the stem.

- Don't use garden shears. These can pinch the branch in a way that hinders healing and future growth.

- If possible, don't harvest branches in damp weather, as this exposes the tree to more mold and bacteria than in dry weather.

- Don't take more than you need. Keep in mind the other living creatures that rely on the trees' blossoms, leaves, shade, etc. for their well-being.

Do:

- Research when the best time is to harvest the species you want to work with in terms of minimizing damage. For example, in four-season climates, spring is best for some trees, while fall is best for others. Work with the trees' natural rhythms as much as possible.

- Keep cutting tools sharp to avoid making ragged cuts that make it harder for the wound to heal.

- And be sure to clean them after harvesting to avoid spreading diseases among trees.

- Cut branches as close to the base as you can, and perpendicular to the branch collar (the "joint" where the branch attaches to the trunk, or to its parent branch).

- Communicate respectfully and lovingly with the tree before, during, and after the harvesting process. See the following example ritual for a suggested approach that you can personalize.

A RITUAL FOR
HARMLESS HARVESTING

This simple ritual can be tailored in whatever way suits your personal approach to magic. Just be sure to remember to respect, protect, and thank the tree.

<u>You will need</u>:

- Cutting tool(s): a boline or other sharp knife, or a saw (if harvesting larger branches)
- An offering for the tree (see suggestions below)
- Cloth bag or other container for the harvested items

<u>Instructions</u>:

Once you've identified the tree you'd like to work with, sit at the base of the tree (or as close as you can get). Greet the tree and talk to it for a little while. You might identify the things you appreciate about—its graceful branches, smooth bark, bright leaves, etc. (Note that this is something you can do ahead of time, or any time you come across a tree that seems to have a special energy about it. No need to limit your communications to just when you need something!) Talk about the spellwork you're preparing for, why you're working it, and what you wish to achieve.

When you feel ready, ask the tree's permission to harvest what you need (a small branch, a strip of bark, etc.) Sit in silence, breathing deeply, and listen with your intuitive mind for the answer. If you feel the tree is saying "no," simply thank it for its response and move on. You can then find another tree and repeat the process. It's important that you honor the "no" rather than overriding it.

The tree may be experiencing challenges to its overall health that would be exacerbated by your cutting something from it. Alternatively, it may be gently trying to tell you that you haven't thought your magical plans through sufficiently. If you keep getting a "no" from several trees, you may want to reevaluate the planned spell or even the goal itself.

If the tree does grant permission, take a deep breath in, and on the exhale visualize a protective white light infusing and surrounding the tree, so that it will not be harmed from your harvesting. Say the following (or similar) words:

"With pure intentions and deepest love, I gratefully accept the gifts of this (name of tree). May the God and Goddess protect this (name of tree) from harm and keep it in good health. So let it be."

Now, using your cutting instrument, harvest only what you need as quickly and cleanly as possible.

Place the leaves, bark, etc. in the bag or other container, and close your eyes for a moment while you once more visualize the tree radiating with white light. See it in complete and vibrant health. Then say the following (or similar) words of thanks:

"I give thanks to you, (name of tree) and wish you health and vitality in all the seasons to come. Blessed Be."

Finally, leave an offering of some kind as a way of thanking the tree. There are many different traditions regarding what to leave for any given type of tree, but some of the more common offerings include small crystals, shiny new coins, a few splashes of wine or milk, small fruits, herbs, honey, and small handfuls of grain. Some contemporary Witches prefer to bring water, which a tree can actually make use of, or even fertilizer. As with all things, follow your intuition when contemplating what to bring as an offering.

TREE SPELLS AND CHARMS

The following spells are just a few examples of how you can use the physical aspects of trees in workings for love, abundance, health, and protection.

Quantities are generally not specified in these spells, as tree magic is a particularly individualized form of magic. This is a great chance to practice letting your intuition guide you as to how much to use (in the case of live harvesting, please use as little as possible).

Typically, several options are presented for you to choose from. So allow your practice of tree magic to be a true *practice*—experiment, substitute, record your results, and have fun!

AUTUMN HARVEST
EASY ABUNDANCE SPELL

This spell affirms the abundance of the natural world via the gifts of the trees. It's an "easy" spell in that it calls for only what Nature has already laid out for you (which, in Autumn, is plenty!).

Take a wander through the woods, your yard, or a nearby park and gather your ingredients while enjoying the refreshing air of the season. You might try incorporating this ritual into your Mabon and/or Samhain celebrations.

<u>You will need:</u>

- At least 7 items from the following (include as many of the trees as possible):
    - Ash seed pods

- - Pine, cedar, and/or fir cones (or any cones from conifers)
  - Maple seeds ("samaras," also known as "helicopters")
  - Acorns
  - Oak leaves
  - Holly berries
- Wand
- Work candle for atmosphere

Instructions:

Light the candle. Spread the items from your "harvest" out on the altar in a visually pleasing arrangement. (Enjoy being creative with this step!) When you're satisfied with your work, pick up your wand and gently touch each tree-gift as you say the following (or similar) words:

"Easy abundance flows through me as it flows through the tree."

When you've touched the wand to all of the gifts, draw a pentacle over the altar and close the spell with the following (or similar) words:

"I bask in the ease and energy of abundance.
Blessed Be."

Leave the arrangement on the altar overnight, or for as long as you continue to feel fresh magical energy from it.

The following day, or once you detect that the spell's energy is beginning to fade from the items, choose one acorn or cone to keep on your altar or carry with you.

Return the rest of the arrangement to the Earth, in affirmation of your part in the natural flow of abundance.

WARM HEALTHY WINTER HEARTH SPELL

Enjoy the quiet and restful energies of winter in good health and warm surroundings with this bundle charm. It's ideal to work this spell in front of an actual fire, so if you have a fire pit or an indoor fireplace, take advantage of it. However, you can create the semblance of a fire with several candles of varying sizes and heights burning close to each other (be careful not to let the flames touch each other).

Gather your twigs on a sunny day (even if it's cold out). You can focus on just one tree type for this spell, or incorporate two or more, according to your preferences and what's available in your area. Conifers are the traditional "winter" trees for this kind of working. Rowan, yew & oak bring in further energies of protection, strength, and healing.

<u>You will need</u>:

- 11 (ideally already-fallen) twigs from one or more of the following trees:
  - Cedar
  - Fir
  - Pine
  - Holly
  - Yew
  - Rowan
  - Oak
- Several inches of strong ribbon, twine, or thin rope
- Scissors
- Bonfire, hearth fire, or several candles

<u>Instructions:</u>

Light the fire (or candles) and sit facing the flames.

Gather the twigs together in a neat bundle and bind them by wrapping the ribbon around them once at one end and tying a knot.

Wrap the ribbon nine more times along the length of the bundle, and tie another knot at the other end.

Cut away any excess ribbon.

Hold the bundle in both hands and say the following (or similar) words:

*"Heat and light of fire, comfort of warmth and health
are with me all this winter long.
Blessed Be."*

Keep the bundle near your hearth or stove (or another focal point of warmth in your home).

In the spring, unwind the ribbon and burn the twigs in a bonfire with a few words of gratitude for any and all good fortune you experienced over the winter. Or, sprinkle the twigs back around the area(s) where you got them. (Don't burn the bundle if it contains yew wood.)

"BACK TO NATURE" SPIRIT CHARM

For people who love being outdoors and connecting with the spiritual energies of the natural world, coming back to "real life" can be a drag. This charm can help you keep some of that high-vibrational natural energy with you in your daily life.

This version uses the traditional Celtic fairy triad, but feel free to use a triad of *any* trees you resonate with personally. For example, you might use birch, willow, & elm to emphasize the energy of the Divine Feminine. Alternatively, gather shed bark, berries, or cones from three different trees you encounter when hiking or biking.

This work should be done outdoors from start to finish, but if that isn't possible, at least take the finished charm outside to charge it with Nature's energy while you say your spell words.

You will need:

- Shed bark and/or twigs from ash, oak, and hawthorn (or trees of your choice)
- Small drawstring bag
- Work candle for atmosphere (optional)

Instructions:

Light the candle, if using. Lay out each piece of bark, twig, etc. in a circle around the drawstring bag.

One at a time, starting at the top and working sunwise (clockwise), pick up each item and hold it between your palms.

Close your eyes, breathe in, and visualize yourself suffused with the beautiful energy of places you love in nature. Note any subtle energetic shifts that take place from your contact with this small piece of the tree.

Give gratitude to the tree it came from, then add it to the bag. When you're finished, close the bag, hold it next to your heart, and say the following (or similar) words:

"Spirits of the Earth and wood,
your light does me the greatest good.
Be with me as I make my way
through indoor spaces, day to day
until I'm free to roam again.
So let it be."

Keep the charm where you'll have ready access to it, in an indoor space you inhabit frequently (such as your desk drawer at work, or the room in your home you spend most of your time in).

Get it out and hold it in your hands when you want to reconnect with the magical vibrations of Nature.

"BUILD YOUR OWN" PROTECTION WITCH JAR

This Witch Jar can be an all-purpose protection spell, or can be tailored to emphasize a specific need. Chief protective uses are listed below. To incorporate the energies of sacred numbers, choose at least 3, but ideally 7 or 9 trees to work with.

"Adjunct" refers to ingredients that lend power to the other ingredients, but are not particularly strong on their own for this purpose.

<u>You will need</u>:

- At least 3, but ideally 7-9 of the following:

- o   Ash bark and/or leaves (travel, especially on or near water, illness)
- o   Holly leaves, and/or twigs (bad luck, evil spirits, lightning)
- o   Rowan leaves and/or twigs (negative vibrations)
- o   Hawthorn (negative vibrations, lightning)
- o   Birch bark, and/or twigs (negative energy & psychic attack)
- o   Dried slippery elm bark (malicious gossip)
- o   Cedar leaves (general psychic protection)
- o   Oak (general protection)
- o   Pine (general protection)
- o   Yew bark (use with caution) (general, adjunct)
- o   Fir (general, adjunct)
- Mortar & pestle
- Small wide-mouthed glass jar with lid
- Maple syrup (or honey)
- 1 black or white spell candle

Instructions:

With your fingers, break up ingredients as necessary into small enough pieces for mixing together.

Add the ingredients one by one to the mortar and stir them 5 times sunwise (clockwise) with the pestle. As you do so, visualize yourself, and your home and family (if applicable) protected by a shield of white light.

Pour the tree mixture into the jar, and pour the maple syrup over it until the mixture is covered.

Close the jar and set the candle on top. Light the candle and let a few drops of the wax melt onto the center of the lid to form a small pool. Press the bottom of the candle into the melted wax and hold it steady until the wax cools enough to keep the candle in place.

Speak a few words relevant to your purpose, affirming that you (and your home and family, if applicable) are protected. Close your spell with "*And so it is*" (or similar words).

Leave the candle to burn all the way down. Keep the jar in a place relevant to your specific protective purpose—your home, your car, your work space, etc.

SPELL FOR WELCOMING LOVE INTO YOUR HOME

This spell is for bringing the energy of love into your life. You can work it for romantic love, but it also applies to the love of family or new friends. It's about cultivating the experience of having love for others and allowing yourself to be loved. In fact, resonating with the vibrational frequency of any form of love will open up the pathways to bring other forms in as well.

You will need:

- 3 or 4 tablespoons of maple syrup
- Small chips of birch, willow, hawthorn, and/or elm bark
- Hawthorn flowers (if available and if working for serious romantic love)
- Holly leaves and/or berries (optional)

Instructions:

Add the dry ingredients one by one to the mortar and stir them three times sunwise (clockwise) with the pestle.

Spoon in the maple syrup (enough so that the consistency of the mixture is mostly liquid) and stir again three times. Spoon a tiny bit more syrup onto the index finger of your dominant hand and eat it. Then say the following (or similar) words:

"Love is infinite and everywhere.
I now draw infinite love into my life.
So let it be."

Dig a small hole in your yard or in a pot of soil near your front door. Pour the mixture into the hole and cover it with soil. The spell will permeate the ground around your home, drawing the experience of love into your life.

ARBOREAL CRAFTING

Here are a few ideas for those who love a keep-it-simple, DIY approach to magic. Let them inspire your own personal practice! And always remember to use caution when working with carving and cutting instruments, as well as incense and essential oils.

MAKING YOUR OWN WAND

Making a wand for use in ritual and magic can be a simple process or an elaborate affair, depending on your preferences. Some Witches like to have a finely polished branch with ornate carvings and crystals at the tip, while others feel more comfortable with something that could easily pass for a plain old twig.

You may want to experiment for awhile as you hone your wand-making skills. Gather several random small branches from the ground so you can try different options. For example, sand one branch and merely remove the bark from another. Then take turns holding each one in your dominant hand. Which one feels more powerful?

You can use the ritual outlined above for harvesting a branch to make a wand from, using a boline in keeping with tradition. Or, you can look for already-fallen branches in the vicinity of the tree you wish to use. (If you want a wide selection to choose from, head out after a storm!) This is a good option for those who would like to try working with a few different types of trees to see which energies they resonate with most.

You can also simply ask the Universe to bring you a perfect branch for your wand. If you do, you will likely find that a branch literally makes its way to your front door, or suddenly appears in your path while you're out walking!

When it comes to length, it is said that wands traditionally run from the crook of your elbow to the end of your forefinger or middle finger. However, many people find this to be impractical and will go for something more in the range of 9 to 12 inches. This is another opportunity to experiment—try out a few different lengths with your "practice sticks" before making your decision.

Thickness is also a matter of preference, and may depend on whether you want to hold the wand with your whole hand or just between your thumb and forefinger. Ideally, one end of the branch will be wider than the other so that the base of the wand is easily distinguishable from the tip. You may find a branch that already has such a shape, or you can shape it yourself by whittling one end down to a graceful point.

Sanding, carving symbols, and adding crystals or other ornamentations can make your wand a one-of-a-kind creation, but these steps are never strictly necessary. (Most Witches at least remove the bark from their wands, but if leaving it on fits your style, then by all means do so.)

No matter what degree of effort you put into it, however, it's important to approach the task with reverence and focus. Make a ritual of the process—light a candle, burn some incense or essential oils, or even cast a circle before beginning.

When the wand is finished, be sure to consecrate it and charge it with your personal magical energy. You can also anoint it with magical oils (tree-based essential oils like cedar, pine, and juniper are particularly appropriate).

Finally, be sure to spend time with your new wand, as it usually takes awhile (some say years!) before your connection with it can reach its full power. Hold it while meditating, use it to cast your ritual circle, keep it near your bed while you sleep, and even just carry it with you when you're puttering around the house. The more you bond energetically with your wand, the stronger its alignment with your magical work will be.

GREEN MAN / WOMAN LEAF "CROWN"

Autumn leaves present a wonderful opportunity to work creatively with Nature in many ways.

This magical headdress can be worn in celebration of Mabon or Samhain, depending on when peak leaf season hits your area. It's also a great "costume" for Witches who want to dress up for Halloween and express an aspect of their true selves at the same time. And it can be a fun project to do with kids! You can also make a summer version with just green leaves.

Look for leaves and boughs that have come off due to wind, or snip some leaves (but first please review the information on harvesting in this section).

For best results, try to gather your leaves no more than three days before you plan to wear the headdress, and don't assemble it until the day or day before. Leaves begin to lose their vitality once they've left the tree, so the longer they sit, the less vibrant and pliable they will appear in the finished piece.

The leaves need to have at least an inch of stem, so not all tree types will work, but oak and maple leaves in particular should be a safe bet.

(Note: the "crown" is actually made of separate pieces that you'll work into your hair, so your hair needs to be long enough to hold clips, bobby pins, or barrettes.)

You will need:

- 15-40 fresh fall leaves
- Twist ties or small rubber bands
- Several hair clips and/or bobby pins

- 1 or more large coffee table books (or other flat, smooth, heavy objects)
- 1 or more candles (optional)
- Mirror

Instructions:

First, gather your leaves. If you're creating the autumn version, this can be the most enjoyable part of the process, as it requires you to start paying close attention to the colors of the trees as the season gets underway. This can be a great excuse for a trip to the park, the woods, or anywhere else that might provide a spectacular variety of leaves to choose from.

Look for the brightest, most blemish-free leaves you can find, and get as many different colors and shades as you can find. Include lots of red, orange, and yellow, but don't leave out greens or vibrant browns if you come across them.

You'll need about 15 leaves at a minimum, but don't be afraid to gather more than you need (unless you're making a summer version and harvesting living leaves). The more you gather now, the better selection you'll have to choose from when you assemble the headdress.

When you have your leaves, spread them out on a table or the floor, and sort them by color. For best results, sort them again by individual shades of color, as if you're creating a painter's palette.

Identify any leaves that have blemishes, tears, or missing points, etc. and put them aside. (Depending on how many leaves you have left, you may want to do another round or two of culling—it's easy to get over-enthusiastic during the gathering process!) If you like, you can use these leaves as seasonal altar decorations or return them to the Earth.

Create 4-6 leaf "bouquets" from the leaves that remain, using 1-2 leaves per color pile. For best appearance, place all leaves face up, and arrange the biggest leaves at the back with smaller leaves in front. Pull the leaves in the center off to each side a bit, so that each leaf can be seen as much as possible. Have fun creating these, and allow your inner artist to guide you! When you're satisfied with each "bouquet," use a twist-tie or rubber band to hold the leaf stems together.

Place the leaf bundles between two flat surfaces, such as two large coffee table books (or on a table, under a book) until you're ready to wear the headdress. (Note: you can also store the leaves this way overnight before bundling them, if you need to take the project in steps.) This will keep the leaves from drying out and curling, and will slow the fading process.

When you're ready to put on your leaf crown, get the bundles back out, and gather your hair clips and/or bobby pins. (Depending on the length and thickness of your hair, you may need more than one clip/pin for each leaf bundle.) Light a candle or two, if you'd like.

Charge the bundled leaves with words of gratitude for the trees you have worked with to create this delightful craft. You might say something like the following:

"As the seasons turn, I thank you, trees, for allowing me to share in your beauty."

Using a mirror to guide you, clip the first leaf bundle to the back of your head, so that the leaves face forward and are mostly above the crown of your head. (If you have long hair, it works best to tie it in a low ponytail at the back of your neck first.) Now clip a bundle to either side of the first one, so that the leaves fan out and no space is visible between them.

Clip the remaining bundles on each side of your head, lying flat on the top of your head, and/or wherever else they fit best, in order to create the image of the Green Man/Woman. Use bobby pins to secure any stray leaf stems (and bring them with you in case you need to make adjustments, especially if you're out on a windy night!)

When you're finished wearing the crown, you can use the leaf bundles as altar decorations for Mabon or Samhain, or just return them to the Earth.

TREE-BASED INCENSE

Making incense can be a somewhat complex affair, depending on the style you want to make (cone, stick/wand, or loose) and how many ingredients you want to include.

Typically, incense blends involve some tree-based ingredients as well as herbs, resins, and/or essential oils. However, a single-ingredient incense also works well as an adjunct to ritual and spellwork.

Below are a few single-tree incenses that require charcoal in order to ignite. (All of these can also be used in blends.) You can find plenty of instructions for making all kinds of incense, online and in print sources (such as Scott Cunningham's *Complete Book of Incense, Oils & Brews*).

- **Birch:** burn the bark for purification, especially after illness

- **Cedar:** burn cedar smudge wands or loose cedar bark chips to purify and consecrate sacred space

- **Fir:** burn the needles to lift depression and clear out negative energy from a space

- **Oak:** burn chips of oak bark for prosperity and/or use it as a base for an incense blend

- **Pine:** burn the needles for purification, healing, and to attract money.

- **Rowan:** burn dried leaves, bark, or berries for protection and to increase psychic awareness

TREE-BASED
MAGICAL OILS AND ESSENCES

Many trees contain aromatic properties that make for wonderfully rich essential oils. There aren't many synergistic combinations of tree oils, however, so here we'll focus on single-oil uses.

For trees that don't have essential oils, you can try tree essences, typically made from either the bark or the blossoms and containing very high vibrations. These can be taken internally, added to magical baths, sprinkled on magical charms, and even used to anoint candles.

- **Birch ("sweet birch"):** purification, healing, fertility

- **Cedar ("cedarwood"):** banishing, good health, connection with divine energy

- **Fir:** prosperity, vitality, Yule celebrations

- **Pine:** purification, banishing, fertility

CONCLUSION

Hopefully you have gained from these pages a greater appreciation for the incredible beings we call trees. Whether you're on a hike, sitting in a park, or simply driving through the suburbs, you will ideally never see the trees around you quite the way you did before.

Working with trees is a uniquely rich form of magic, as it can be done anytime you're simply in the presence of a tree, even if there are other, non-magical people around. A soft, intentional touch of your hand to a leaf or trunk is an opportunity to exchange energy with a magical being, with no one nearby even noticing.

As you continue to develop your practice and deepen your relationship with specific kinds of trees, you may also want to incorporate trees into your life in new ways. Perhaps you'd like to study the Ogham, starting with the letters named for trees featured in this guide. Or you might learn one or more of the ancient runic systems and make your own set of runes from the branch of a tree growing near you.

If you're blessed with property of your own, consider planting and tending a sacred grove of trees that will grow well in your area. You can also volunteer to plant trees with an environmental organization, and dedicate your effort to the well-being of the Earth.

No matter where you go from here, may your path be blessed with the presence of beautiful, sheltering, abundant, magical trees!

SUGGESTIONS FOR FURTHER READING

Working with trees in your practice of the Craft can be a lifelong journey, as there is no end to what trees can teach us about the inherent magic of the Universe. Here are just a few suggestions for expanding your knowledge of trees and tree magic.

The tree identification guides included here cover all of North America, but there are also many guides for individual regions and even states, which may provide information on more species near you.

Happy reading!

Tree Symbolism, Lore, and Magic:

Danu Forest, *Celtic Tree Magic: Ogham Lore and Druid Mysteries* (2014)

Fred Hageneder, *The Meaning of Trees* (2005)

Ellen Evert Hopman, *Tree Medicine, Tree Magic* (1991)

Sandra Kynes, *Whispers from the Woods: The Lore & Magic of Trees* (2006)

Tess Whitehurst, *The Magic of Trees: A Guide to Their Sacred Wisdom & Metaphysical Properties* (2017)

Magical Crafting with Trees:

Scott Cunningham *The Complete Book of Incense, Oils & Brews* (1989)

Alferian Gwydion MacLir, *Wandlore: The Art of Crafting the Ultimate Magical Tool* (2011)

Gypsey Elaine Teague, *The Witch's Guide to Wands: A Complete Botanical, Magical, and Elemental Guide to Making, Choosing, and Using the Right Wand* (2015)

Tree Identification Guides:

C. Frank Brockman, *Trees of North America: A Guide to Field Identification, Revised and Updated* (2002)

Bland Crowder, *National Geographic Pocket Guide to Trees and Shrubs of North America* (2015)

Keith Rushforth, *National Geographic Field Guide to the Trees of North America: The Essential Identification Guide for Novice and Expert* (2006)

TABLE OF CORRESPONDENCE: TREES

Tree	Magical Uses	Gender
Ash	Protection, prosperity, healing, wisdom, spiritual growth	Masculine, Feminine
Birch	Purification, illumination, beginnings, renewal, love, beauty, protection	Feminine
Cedar	Renewal, rejuvenation, protection, purification, luck, health, prosperity, banishing	Masculine
Elm	Love, protection, stability, nature spirits, divine feminine, fertility	Feminine
Fir	Healing, regeneration, childbirth, youth, vitality, prosperity, change	Feminine
Hawthorn	Fertility, purity, marriage, protection, patience, confidence, creativity	Feminine
Holly	Balance, positive energy, love, attraction, fertility, victory, protection, nature spirits	Masculine, Feminine
Maple	Travel, beauty, love, joy, prosperity, abundance, creativity, communication	Feminine, Masculine
Oak	Strength, prosperity, fertility, courage, wisdom, longevity, abundance, truth, protection, good fortune	Masculine
Pine	Longevity, renewal, health, strength, fertility, prosperity, purification, good fortune, protection	Masculine, Feminine
Rowan (Mountain Ash)	Psychic abilities, healing, positivity, protection, strength, power, insight, nature spirits	Masculine
Willow	Renewal, immortality, healing grief, vitality, lunar magic, change, love, psychic abilities	Feminine
Yew	Knowledge, wisdom, spiritual growth, protection, transformation, psychic abilities, strength, rebirth	Feminine

Tree	Elements	Zodiac	Zodiac	Special Notes
Ash	Fire, Air, Water	Sun, Neptune	Pisces, Aries	
Birch	Air, Water, Fire	Venus	Sagittarius	
Cedar	Fire, Earth, Air	Sun, Jupiter, Mars, Mercury	Leo, Gemini, Virgo	
Elm	Air, Water, Earth	Mercury, Saturn	Capricorn, Pisces	
Fir	Earth	Moon, Jupiter, Pluto	Capricorn, Cancer	Some species poisonous to animals. Oil can irritate skin.
Hawthorn	Water, Air, Earth	Mars	Taurus, Cancer	
Holly	Fire	Mars, Saturn	Leo, Sagittarius	Can be toxic to humans and animals.
Maple	Water, Earth	Moon, Jupiter, Neptune	Libra, Virgo	
Oak	Water, Earth, Air	Jupiter, Mars, Sun	Leo	
Pine	Air, Fire, Earth	Mars, Jupiter, Saturn	Cancer, Capricorn	
Rowan (Mountain Ash)	Fire	Sun, Mercury, Uranus	Aquarius	Berries can be toxic when raw.
Willow	Water	Moon	Cancer, Scorpio	
Yew	Earth, Water	Saturn, Pluto, Jupiter	Scorpio	All parts toxic, use with care.

THREE FREE
AUDIOBOOK PROMOTION

Don't forget, you can now enjoy **three audiobooks completely free of charge** when you start a free 30-day trial with Audible.

If you're new to the Craft, *Wicca Starter Kit* contains three of Lisa's most popular books for beginning Wiccans. You can download it for free at:

www.wiccaliving.com/free-wiccan-audiobooks

Or, if you're wanting to expand your magical skills, check out *Spellbook Starter Kit,* with three collections of spellwork featuring the powerful energies of candles, colors, crystals, mineral stones, and magical herbs. Download over 150 spells for free at:

www.wiccaliving.com/free-spell-audiobooks

Members receive free audiobooks every month, as well as exclusive discounts. And, if you don't want to continue with Audible, just remember to cancel your membership. You won't be charged a cent, and you'll get to keep your books!

Happy listening!

MORE BOOKS BY
LISA CHAMBERLAIN

Wicca for Beginners: A Guide to Wiccan Beliefs, Rituals, Magic, and Witchcraft

Wicca Book of Spells: A Book of Shadows for Wiccans, Witches, and Other Practitioners of Magic

Wicca Herbal Magic: A Beginner's Guide to Practicing Wiccan Herbal Magic, with Simple Herb Spells

Wicca Book of Herbal Spells: A Book of Shadows for Wiccans, Witches, and Other Practitioners of Herbal Magic

Wicca Candle Magic: A Beginner's Guide to Practicing Wiccan Candle Magic, with Simple Candle Spells

Wicca Book of Candle Spells: A Book of Shadows for Wiccans, Witches, and Other Practitioners of Candle Magic

Wicca Crystal Magic: A Beginner's Guide to Practicing Wiccan Crystal Magic, with Simple Crystal Spells

Wicca Book of Crystal Spells: A Book of Shadows for Wiccans, Witches, and Other Practitioners of Crystal Magic

Tarot for Beginners: A Guide to Psychic Tarot Reading, Real Tarot Card Meanings, and Simple Tarot Spreads

Runes for Beginners: A Guide to Reading Runes in Divination, Rune Magic, and the Meaning of the Elder Futhark Runes

Wicca Moon Magic: A Wiccan's Guide and Grimoire for Working Magic with Lunar Energies

Wicca Wheel of the Year Magic: A Beginner's Guide to the Sabbats, with History, Symbolism, Celebration Ideas, and Dedicated Sabbat Spells

Wicca Kitchen Witchery: A Beginner's Guide to Magical Cooking, with Simple Spells and Recipes

Wicca Essential Oils Magic: A Beginner's Guide to Working with Magical Oils, with Simple Recipes and Spells

Wicca Elemental Magic: A Guide to the Elements, Witchcraft, and Magical Spells

Wicca Magical Deities: A Guide to the Wiccan God and Goddess, and Choosing a Deity to Work Magic With

Wicca Living a Magical Life: A Guide to Initiation and Navigating Your Journey in the Craft

Magic and the Law of Attraction: A Witch's Guide to the Magic of Intention, Raising Your Frequency, and Building Your Reality

Wicca Altar and Tools: A Beginner's Guide to Wiccan Altars, Tools for Spellwork, and Casting the Circle

Wicca Finding Your Path: A Beginner's Guide to Wiccan Traditions, Solitary Practitioners, Eclectic Witches, Covens, and Circles

Wicca Book of Shadows: A Beginner's Guide to Keeping Your Own Book of Shadows and the History of Grimoires

Modern Witchcraft and Magic for Beginners: A Guide to Traditional and Contemporary Paths, with Magical Techniques for the Beginner Witch

FREE GIFT REMINDER

Just a reminder that Lisa is giving away an exclusive, free spell book as a thank-you gift to new readers!

Little Book of Spells contains ten spells that are ideal for newcomers to the practice of magic, but are also suitable for any level of experience.

Read it on read on your laptop, phone, tablet, Kindle or Nook device by visiting:

<u>www.wiccaliving.com/bonus</u>

DID YOU ENJOY
WICCA TREE MAGIC?

Thanks so much for reading this book! I know there are many great books out there about Wicca, so I really appreciate you choosing this one.

If you enjoyed the book, I have a small favor to ask—would you take a couple of minutes to leave a review for this book on Amazon?

Your feedback will help me to make improvements to this book, and to create even better ones in the future. It will also help me develop new ideas for books on other topics that might be of interest to you. Thanks in advance for your help!

Made in the USA
Monee, IL
08 September 2020

41751665R00080